SCHOLASTIC

YEAR IN SPORTS 2021

Copyright © 2020 by Shoreline Publishing Group LLC

All rights reserved. Published by Scholastic Inc., *Publishers since 1920*. SCHOLASTIC and associated logos are trademarks and/or registered trademarks of Scholastic Inc.

ISBN: 978-1-338-65471-4

10 9 8 7 6 5 4 3 2 1   20 21 22 23 24

Printed in the U.S.A.   40
First edition, December 2020

Produced by Shoreline Publishing Group LLC

Due to the publication date, records, results, and statistics are current as of mid-July 2020.

UNAUTHORIZED: This book is not sponsored by or affiliated with the athletes, teams, or anyone involved with them.

Contents

Timeout!

Every sport has timeouts. (Yes, we see you, soccer, but you have water breaks now!) In 2020, the whole world took one big timeout. The COVID-19 pandemic started raging in February and quickly changed everyday life just about everywhere in the world. In the world of sports, it was clear early on things would have to change or stop all together. Scientists said the virus spread easily in large gatherings of people. Sports, of course, are all about large gatherings of people, indoors and out.

Then on March 11, **Rudy Gobert** of the Utah Jazz was diagnosed with the virus. The game he was about to play in was cancelled. The NBA soon stopped the whole season. Just about every sport soon followed in one way or the other.

On March 24, the Summer Olympics, set to start on July 23 in Tokyo, were postponed to 2021.

And just like that, the *Year in Sports* got pretty short! Of course, it was the right thing to do. The safety and health of fans, stadium workers, players, coaches, referees—even mascots!—is more important than winning or losing a game.

Athletes headed home and worked out in private. Coaches headed home to spend time with families they usually missed when they were on the road. Fans stayed

Masks on! Sports covered up for COVID.

safe with their families and watched old sports events or even read more books! (Thank you, readers!) It was a scary time and people missed the comfort of sports.

But it had to be done.

As the weeks and months went on, people in the sports world came through in the clutch, just like they do on the court or on the field. They helped! Check out pages 6-7 for some of the ways that your favorite stars showed that they were all-stars off the field, too.

The Mystics were champs before the Big Timeout!

In the meantime, with sports in The Big Timeout, how did we fill up this book? Well, we were lucky that lots of the big events we cover were already completed. So, inside you'll read about the surprising World Series win by the Washington Nationals. Check out another first-time winner, the WNBA's Washington Mystics. The Kansas City Chiefs didn't win their first Super Bowl, but they took 50 years to win their second! We also report on the end of the 2019 NASCAR, Formula 1, and other motor sports seasons.

Since so many sports did not happen, we were able to take some time (and more than 60 pages!) to look back an amazing Decade in Sports: the 2010s. Starting on page 124, you'll find 10 years of memories, heroes, highlights, championships, and more. How many do you remember? How many did you watch? What were your favorite 2010s memories?

Sports, like everything else, will be back. In fact, some of the sports we love were starting to come back in late summer and fall. That's great news for next year's YEAR IN SPORTS!

COVID-19: Sports Help Out

Sports started stopping in mid-March. Within days, athletes from around the world began donating money to help people who lost their jobs when the games were postponed. As the crisis went on, teams, leagues, athletes, and others in sports chipped in generously. We can't list them all, but here are some highlights.

✻ NBA stars like **Kevin Love** and **Giannis Antetokounmpo** donated hundreds of thousands of dollars for basketball arena workers. Rookie star **Zion Williamson** promised to pay the salaries of every worker at the New Orleans Pelicans' arena for a month! Utah's **Rudy Gobert** not only suffered through the virus, he donated $500,000!

✻ As the weeks went on, people started to need help getting food. When businesses closed, millions of people were without jobs, money, or food. **Russell Wilson** of the Seattle Seahawks was one of many stars who chipped in to help. He donated a million meals to a food bank. **J. J. Watt** of the Houston Texans sent more than $350,000 to a Houston charity. Super Bowl champ **Patrick Mahomes** made sure that schoolchildren in Kansas City had enough to eat.

✻ **Drew Brees** has thrilled New Orleans Saints fans for years. He thrilled them again when he and his wife Brittany donated $5 million to Louisiana to help with meal programs for children, families, and senior citizens.

✻ A two-sport family chipped in. **Zach Ertz** is a Pro Bowl tight end

Carlos Correa

The Ertzes sent their love to Philly fans.

Zion dunked into his wallet to help out!

in. And every team in MLB donated $1 million each (some teams did much more) to help pay stadium workers sent home when no games were played.

✳ The crisis hit countries around the world, of course. Soccer superstars **Cristiano Ronaldo** and **Lionel Messi** have a long rivalry on the field. They put that aside to each pledge more than $1 million to help hospitals in Spain. **Bismack Biyombo** of the NBA's Charlotte Hornets is from the Democratic Republic of the Congo. He sent $1 million back home to buy medical and safety supplies.

with the Eagles. **Julie Ertz** is a World Cup-winning U.S. pro soccer player. They donated to help Philadelphia food banks.

✳ **Carlos Correa**, the Astros' star shortstop, sent $500,000 to the city of Houston to help with relief efforts. Dozens of other MLB players chipped

✳ The Athletes Relief online campaign was supported by dozens of stars, including NASCAR's **Jimmie Johnson**, gymnastics hero **Simone Biles**, skateboard legend **Tony Hawk**, softball standout **Jennie Finch**, and many more from around the world.

❝ There are so many things people can do to support those affected right now. Big or small, every donation or act of service goes a long way. ❞

– WNBA MVP ELENA DELLE DONNE

Black Lives Matter
The Sports World Says "Yes!"

On May 25, 2020, a Black man named George Floyd was murdered by a police officer in Minneapolis. The event was caught on video and seen around the world. Almost overnight, a massive movement rose up to demand an end to the racism that led to Floyd's death—and that of many other Black people. It's a huge and important story and you should read about it. Here, we highlight just a few of the ways that the sports world stepped up to support the movement and help lead the way to change.

❝ Right now, more than any other time in my lifetime, it feels like we have the ability to literally turn away from the systems that we've had for centuries, and actually start over. ❞
—NEW ORLEANS SAINTS S **MALCOLM JENKINS**

More than 70 people from the Denver Broncos—including star LB **Von Miller** (above), the team's head coach and owner—led a march in their home city, drawing tens of thousands of people to their side.

NBA star **Russell Westbrook** spoke at a Black Lives Matter rally near Los Angeles. "Protect your family," he said. "In times like these, we need to stick together."

Tennis star **Coco Gauff** is only 16, but she made her voice heard loud and clear at a rally in Florida.

College athletes from all over took part in marches and events. Oklahoma State RB **Chuba Hubbard** called for his coach to apologize for wearing a shirt that promoted a website that "called Black Lives Matter a 'farce.'" Coach **Mike Gundy** apologized.

The protests were worldwide. When soccer's English Premier League restarted, all the players wore "BLACK LIVES MATTER" on their jerseys in place of their names. They took a knee as each game started to show their support for antiracism. Leagues in Germany, Italy, and other countries also showed that they were in the fight, too.

Megastar **LeBron James** announced that he was forming a new organization to promote voting rights and to encourage people to get out and vote for change.

NASCAR's **Bubba Wallace**, the only current African-American driver, demanded that Confederate flags be removed from race locations. The flag was often seen at the track, and it remains a symbol of a racist past to many. NASCAR banned the flags for good.

WNBA star **Renee Montgomery** believes the need for change is so great, she is giving up her 2020 season to work for the cause.

The 2019–2020 LUCKY SEVEN

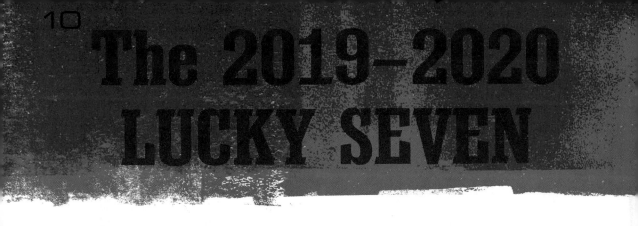

Normally, this section would be our Top 10—the 10 best, most important, most memorable, most incredible events in sports for an entire year. Well, that won't work, for obvious reasons. So we'll call this our Lucky Seven: the best from the sports that were completed before the end of March 2020. It's still a pretty great collection of memories and moments. See if your favorites made the list!

7 **AUSSIE RULERS** *Nearly all the men's and women's tennis and golf Grand Slam events were canceled or postponed. However, one Grand Slam tennis tournament did finish Down Under.* **Novak Djokovic** *won the men's title at the Australian Open, giving him an incredible eight Aussie titles (and 17 Grand Slam trophies in his career, third-most ever). That's the new Aussie record Meanwhile,* **Sofia Kenin** *of the US won her first-ever Grand Slam in the women's singles event.*

6

YOU GO, JOE! *Thanks to Q.B. Joe Burrow having perhaps the best season ever in college football history, the LSU Tigers won their fourth national championship. First, they rolled over Ohio State in the semifinal 63–28. Burrow had an incredible seven TD passes in that game, including six in the first half! In the championship game, Burrow had six more to lead LSU to a 42–25 win over Clemson.*

5

MIGHTY MYSTICS Superstar *Elena Delle Donne* (pictured) led the Washington Mystics to the team's first WNBA championship. They beat the Connecticut Sun in a thrilling, five-game Finals. However, it was another Mystics player who was the big hero. *Emma Meesseman* piled on the points when Delle Donne struggled with a back injury. Emma had Elena's back—get it?

4

HIGH FLYER *In late 2019, **Simone Biles** made gymnastics history by becoming the first American to win five World Championships. Her all-time medals total in the event also reached 25, just shy of a new record. Is she the greatest female gymnast of all time? Could be!*

3

NATS WIN! *Who says baseball is a young man's game? The Washington Nationals had the oldest roster of players in the game, but they wound up carrying home the 2019 World Series title. The Nats beat the Houston Astros in seven awesome games. Washington won two, then lost three straight, but rallied to win Games 6 and 7 on the road.*

2

SUPER CHIEFS! *Kansas City had not won a Super Bowl in 50 seasons.* **Patrick Mahomes** *made the 2019 season into a happy anniversary by leading the Chiefs to the team's second-ever NFL title. His powerful passing and creative leadership led K.C. past a very good San Francisco 49ers team 31–20. Running back* **Damien Williams** *scored two late TDs to help clinch the title.*

1 **TIME OUT!** *Well, it was not great, but it was certainly memorable. Beginning with the NBA on March 11, just about every part of the sports world shut down for at least three months because of the COVID-19 pandemic. Players and teams tried to help (see page 6) while they stayed in shape and awaited the day things could start again. Like everyone, sports will take a long time to recover, and we can't wait! Here's hoping we're all cheering again soon.*

SUPER CONFETTI!
The NFL celebrated its 100th birthday in 2019, and the Kansas City Chiefs capped off the celebration with a big win. The Chiefs won their first Super Bowl in 50 years by beating the San Francisco 49ers.

NFL

Happy Birthday, NFL!

The NFL celebrated its 100th season in 2019 and created memories that will last the next 100 years! In 2018, the big new star was Kansas City QB **Patrick Mahomes**. In 2019, it was Baltimore passer **Lamar Jackson**. Actually, not just "passer," but all-around superstar. Jackson set a new all-time record for QBs by rushing for 1,206 yards. He also led the surprising Ravens to the NFL's best record. They fell in the playoffs, but watch for more big plays from Jackson in 2020.

The Patriots relied on a powerful defense to be the AFC's other dominant team. Then a last-game loss to Miami sent them to the wild-card round where they were shocked by the Titans. The Houston Texans lost superstar **J.J. Watt** early in the season, but counted on QB **Deshaun Watson** to lead them to an AFC South title.

In the NFC, San Francisco was the big story. The Niners won only four games in 2018. In 2019, they won 13! It was one of the biggest one-season turnarounds ever. They used a strong running game and one of the league's top defenses to win.

The Green Bay Packers and New Orleans Saints depended on their veteran

> **❝I really want that Super Bowl trophy so badly for Baltimore and the coaching staff and the fans.❞**
>
> — BALTIMORE QB LAMAR JACKSON

THE NFL 100

As part of its celebration of 100 years, the NFL named its NFL 100 All-Time Team, including coaches. Experts looked at thousands of players to come up with the biggest and best names of all time. Four members of the team played or coached in 2019.

- Patriots coach **Bill Belichick**
- Patriots QB **Tom Brady**
- Cardinals WR **Larry Fitzgerald**
- Colts kicker **Adam Vinatieri**

Visit this site to see the whole list. How many NFL 100 people are from your favorite team? nfl.com/100/all-time-team/roster

All season long, the NFL celebrated its amazing past. The many great young players, including Mahomes, Jackson, and Watson, show that the league has a pretty awesome future, too!

QBs—**Aaron Rodgers** and **Drew Brees**. Both led their teams to 13 wins as well but could not make the centennial party in Miami.
The Niners ended up winning the NFC and (remember him?) Mahomes led the Chiefs to the AFC title.

Drew Brees, record-setter—see page 29!

2019 Final Regular-Season Standings

AFC EAST		AFC NORTH		AFC SOUTH		AFC WEST	
Patriots	12–4	Ravens	14–2	Texans	10-6	Chiefs	12–4
Bills	10–6	Steelers	8–8	Titans	9–7	Broncos	7–9
Jets	7–9	Browns	6–10	Colts	7–9	Raiders	7–9
Dolphins	5–11	Bengals	2–14	Jaguars	6–10	Chargers	5–11
NFC EAST		**NFC NORTH**		**NFC SOUTH**		**NFC WEST**	
Eagles	9–7	Packers	13–3	Saints	13–3	49ers	13–3
Cowboys	8–8	Vikings	10–6	Falcons	7–9	Seahawks	11–5
Giants	4–12	Bears	8–8	Buccaneers	7–9	Rams	9–7
Washington	3–13	Lions	3–12-1	Panthers	5–11	Cardinals	5–10-1

1st Quarter
WEEKS 1-4

Giants QB Daniel Jones

WEEK 1

✱ Ravin' About a Raven: QB **Lamar Jackson** posted a perfect 158.3 passer rating while leading his Baltimore Ravens to a shocking 59–10 win over the Miami Dolphins. Jackson equaled a team record with 5 TD passes. The team's 59 points and 643 total yards were other all-time Ravens marks.

✱ Comebacks Galore: Three teams pulled off big comebacks in the season's first week. Top rookie **Kyler Murray** had a poor start but finished strong. He threw two

TDs in the fourth quarter to help his Arizona Cardinals tie the Detroit Lions after trailing by 18 points. The Philadelphia Eagles were behind Washington by 13 in the second quarter. **DeSean Jackson** caught a pair of scores for Philly and the Eagles won 32-27. And the Buffalo Bills were down 16-0 to the New York Jets but scored 17 points in a row to earn a one-point win.

WEEK 2

✱ Three for Two: The New England Patriots shut out the Miami Dolphins 43–0. That put the total of points allowed by the Pats D at a total of three after two games (they allowed just 3 points in Week 1). That's the fewest points allowed after a team's first pair of games since 1981!

✱ Falcons Fly: On a fourth-and-three late in the game, Atlanta's **Julio Jones** caught a short pass and turned it into a win for the Falcons. He ran 54 yards to the end zone for the TD that put his team ahead of the Philadelphia Eagles to stay. Atlanta won 24–20.

✱ Ouch: Two big-name QBs both went down with injuries and to make things worse, both of their teams lost. **Drew Brees** of the Saints hurt his thumb early in his team's 27–9 loss to the LA Rams. Pittsburgh's **Ben Roethlisberger** sat out most of the Steelers' 28–26 loss to Seattle. "Big Ben" later learned he would miss the rest of the 2019 season with his elbow injury.

✱ It Just Takes One (Second):

Chicago's 2018 season ended with a missed kick in the playoffs. The Bears won their first game of 2019 by making a huge kick. After officials put one second back on the clock following a long pass, Chicago's **Eddy Piñiero** drilled a 53-yard field goal to beat Denver 16–14.

WEEK 3

✱ New Giant in Town: QB **Daniel Jones** was a surprise No. 6 overall draft

pick by the New York Giants in 2019. Before the team's game at Tampa Bay, Giants coaches threw Jones into the fire as the starting QB, replacing **Eli Manning**. Jones responded with a dramatic 18 point comeback, running for two scores and throwing for two more. His seven-yard run with less than two minutes left gave the Giants a 32–31 win.

✱ Break Up the Bills!: Buffalo

moved to 3–0 for the first time since 2011 with a 21–17 win over Cincinnati. QB **Josh Allen** threw for 243 yards and a TD, helped by a big catch-and-run from TE **Dawson Knox**.

✱ Who Needs Drew?: The Saints

were without superstar QB **Drew Brees**, but they looked just fine. Backup Teddy Bridgewater had 2 TD passes and **Deonte Harris** scored on an exciting 53-yard punt return to help New Orleans beat Seattle 33–27.

WEEK 4

✱ Jaguars Roar: Jacksonville RB

Leonard Fournette had a career day while helping his team beat the Denver Broncos 26–24. Fournette rumbled for 225 yards, but it was up to K **Josh Lambo** to

win the game. His 33-yard field goal went through as time ran out!

✱ Chubb Churns: An 88-yard TD run

helped Cleveland RB **Nick Chubb** pile up 165 yards in the Browns' 40–25 defeat of Baltimore. Chubb scored two other times, while QB **Baker Mayfield** threw for 342 yards and a TD.

✱ Chiefs Say "Whew!": Kansas

City remained undefeated after coming back to beat Detroit 34–30, thanks to a TD run by **Darrel Williams** with just 20 seconds left. The 2018 NFL MVP, **Patrick Mahomes**, led his team down the field to the score, including making a key fourth-down run to keep the drive alive.

Fournette's big day set up Lambo.

2nd Quarter
WEEKS 5–8

WEEK 5

✷ Revenge!: In January, the Chiefs beat the Colts in an AFC playoff game. Indianapolis got revenge as October began, beating Kansas City 19–13. The Colts defense mostly shut down the powerful Chiefs offense, led by MVP **Patrick Mahomes**. Indy K **Adam Vinatieri**, the NFL's oldest player at 46, had 4 field goals.

✷ Watson...Wow!: Houston QB **Deshaun Watson** had a huge day, with a career-best 426 passing yards as the

Houston QB Deshaun Watson

Texans beat the Falcons 53–32. Watson's five TD passes, three of which went to **Will Fuller**, tied his career best, too.

✷ Jolly (Roger) Good Show: The Oakland Raiders made the long trip to London to play the Chicago Bears and got to fly home happy. Rookie RB **Josh Jacobs** had two TD runs, including the game-winner with less than two minutes left. Oakland won 24–21.

WEEK 6

✷ Niners!: San Francisco remained the only unbeaten NFC team with a shocking 20–7 win over the Rams—the defending NFC champs. LA star QB **Jared Goff** managed only 78 passing yards. The Rams did not score after their opening drive. That was not a surprise to the Niners D, which came into the game second in the league in fewest points allowed.

✷ Welcome Back, Sam!: Jets QB **Sam Darnold** returned after missing games due to an illness and he led his team to a huge upset over the Cowboys. Darnold threw 2 TDs and the Jets D broke up a last-minute two-point attempt to clinch a 24–22 win.

✷ Panthers on the Prowl: Carolina picked off 5 passes by Tampa Bay's **Jameis Winston** in a 37–26 win in London. They were part of a Panthers-record 7 forced turnovers. As for the offense, RB **Christian McCaffrey** continued his hot start by scoring 2 TDs, which teammate WR **Curtis Samuel** matched.

Surprise star Chase Edmonds had three TDs to power an Arizona win.

WEEK 7

✱ Awesome Aaron:
Green Bay QB **Aaron Rodgers** became the first QB since 1991 to throw 5 TD passes and run for another in one game. His heroics thrilled his fantasy owners and Packers fans as the Packers rolled to a 42–24 win over the Raiders.

✱ Marvelous Marvin:
Detroit WR **Marvin Jones Jr.** caught 4 TD passes from **Matthew Stafford** but it was not enough to beat the Vikings. Minnesota QB **Kirk Cousins** threw 4 TDs of his own in leading his team to a 42–30 win.

✱ Fabulous Fill-in:
Arizona's star RB **David Johnson** was nursing an ankle injury. His sub took advantage! **Chase Edmonds** ran for 126 yards and three TDs, each of which went for 20 or more yards. That was enough for the Cardinals to hand the Giants a 27–21 defeat.

WEEK 8

✱ Shut-Down D:
The Patriots remained the only undefeated team in the AFC with a 27–13 win over the Browns. **Tom Brady** had 2 TD passes, but the story continued to be the Pats D. The team has scored 189 points more than it has given up. That is the most in the NFL after eight games since 1920!

✱ Niners Power:
The 49ers continued their perfect season with a dominating 51–13 win over the Panthers. RB **Tevin Coleman** scored four times. The win made the Niners 7–0 for the first time since 1990.

3rd Quarter
WEEKS 9-12

The Pack's goal-line stop in the snow!

overtime to give the Seahawks a 40–34 win over the surprisingly tough Buccaneers. Seattle QB **Russell Wilson** threw 5 TD passes, tying his career high. The 'Hawks had a chance to win in regulation, but K **Jason Myers** missed a 40-yard FG attempt.

✱ No Mahomes, No Problem:
Kansas City was missing its injured star QB again, but held on to beat Minnesota. K **Harrison Butker** was the star, hitting a career-long-tying 54-yard FG. Then as the clock ran out on the game, his 44-yarder gave the Chiefs a 26–23 win.

WEEK 9

✱ Pats Not Perfect:
New England lost its first game of the year to **Lamar Jackson** and the high-flying Ravens 37–20. Jackson scored two rushing TDs as the Ravens became the first team to find a way through the Patriots' amazing defense. Baltimore also had a 70-yard fumble return TD.

✱ Chargers Shock Pack:
Los Angeles has been struggling this year after reaching the AFC Championship Game last season. They got it together against Green Bay, though, posting a surprising 26–11 win. RB **Melvin Gordon** scored twice and **Michael Badgley** came back from an injury to kick four field goals.

✱ OT + TD = W:
Seattle TE **Jacob Hollister** dove into the end zone in

WEEK 10

✱ Battle of New York:
Even though the Giants QB **Daniel Jones** had 4 TD passes, it was **Sam Darnold** and the Jets who won the Battle of the Big Apple. RB **Le'Veon Bell's** fourth-quarter TD run was the difference in the Jets' 34–27 victory, only their second of the season!

✱ Falcons Fly!:
The Saints were 13.5-point favorites and playing at home, but the Falcons didn't care. They shut down the New Orleans offense, sacking **Drew Brees** six times. **Matt Ryan** had 2 TD passes for the Falcons, who won 26–9.

✱ Stop in the Snow:
A late-game snowstorm didn't stop the Packers. But Green Bay did stop Carolina's **Christian McCaffrey** at the goal line on the game's final play. The defensive stand preserved the Pack's 24–16 win.

★ Block That Kick!: That's just what Tennessee's **Joshua Kalu** did on the final play of his team's surprise 35–32 win over Kansas City. The Titans spoiled the return of KC QB **Patrick Mahomes** from his knee injury. RB **Derrick Henry** led the way with 188 yards rushing and 2 TDs.

WEEK 11

★ 20–0? No Problem: Minnesota trailed Denver by that score at halftime. The second half was a different story. QB **Kirk Cousins** led four straight touchdown drives, while the Vikings defense shut down the Broncos. A 32-yard TD pass to **Kyle Rudolph** put the Vikes up for good in the fourth quarter en route to a 27-23 victory.

★ Another Pats Passer: Tom **Brady** was held without a TD pass by the Eagles, but New England had a backup plan. WR **Julian Edelman** fired a TD pass to **Phillip Dorsett** for a key score in the Pats' 17–10 win. "I'm sure we'll have to ice [Edelman's] shoulder this week," joked Pats coach **Bill Belichick**.

WEEK 12

★ Really Big Score: Tampa Bay beat Atlanta 35–22, but the "really big" news came from nose tackle **Vita Vea** of the Bucs. The 347-pound defender snagged a TD pass from **Jameis Winston**. Vea became the largest NFL player ever to score a TD on offense. Win a trivia contest by learning his full name, thanks to his Samoan background: **Tevita Tuli'aki'ono Tuipulotu Mosese Va'hae Fehoko Faletau Vea.**

★ Good for Gore: Buffalo ran its record to 8–3 with a 20–3 win over

Denver. RB Frank Gore ran pretty well, too. He gained 65 yards to move into third place on the NFL's all-time rushing yards list. Now with 15,289 yards, Gore passed Hall of Famer **Barry Sanders**.

Vita Vea's "big" TD!

4th Quarter

WEEKS 13-17

WEEK 13

★ Watson Plays Catcher: The Texans handed the Patriots their second loss of the season in a big Sunday night game. Houston won 28–22, but it wasn't that close. The Texans dominated the game, thanks to **Deshaun Watson's** 3 TD passes. He also caught his first TD pass on an option pitch from **DeAndre Hopkins**.

★ Super Bowl Preview?: Baltimore took over the No. 1 position in the AFC with the Patriots loss and the Ravens' 20–17

Tennessee QB Ryan Tannehill

win over the 49ers. It was a tight game played in rough weather. Ravens K **Justin Tucker** provided the winning points with a 49-yard field goal as time ran out.

★ Joy in Cincy: The Bengals finally won their first game of the season, beating the Jets 22–6. Cincinnati had gone nearly a year since their last victory. QB **Andy Dalton** returned to lead the team after he was benched for three games.

WEEK 14

★ What a Game!: Two of the NFL's top teams matched up and played one of the highest-scoring and most memorable games of the season. The Saints and 49ers matched touchdowns and field goals over and over. Both QBs had huge games. **Drew Brees** had 5 TD passes and scored himself on a one-yard dive for the Saints. **Jimmy Garoppolo** had 4 TD strikes of his own—and both players had exactly 349 passing yards! New Orleans took the lead with less than a minute to play. But Garoppolo used a long pass to TE **George Kittle** to help set up a game-winning 30-yard field goal; SF won 48–46..

★ Tannehill the Titan: Tennessee continued to roll behind QB **Ryan Tannehill**. He had 3 TD passes in leading his team to a 42–21 win over Oakland. Since taking over for **Marcus Mariota**, **Tannehill** won six of his seven starts and had the highest passer rating in the league over those games.

Fitzgerald led a Miami upset.

WEEK 15

✱ New Rushing Champ:

Baltimore's superstar QB **Lamar Jackson** set a new NFL record for rushing yards in a season. He had 86 yards as his Ravens beat the Jets 42-21 to run his 2019 total to 1,103 yards. Baltimore also clinched the NFC North title and set a new team record for total rushing yards.

✱ 450 x 2: Tampa Bay's **Jameis Winston** had two awesome weeks in a row. Against both the Colts and Lions, he went over 450 yards passing. A big deal? Yes! He was the first NFL passer ever with back-to-back games with that many passing yards. His arm must have been really tired!

✱ Fantastic Falcons Finish:

Atlanta upset the high-flying 49ers with a TD pass with two seconds left. It was first ruled short of the goal line, but then the replay officials reversed the call. To cap things off, Atlanta returned a fumble of the kickoff for another touchdown to make the final score 29–22.

✱ Rams Lassoed: The Rams' faint playoff hopes faded in Dallas. The Cowboys piled up 44 points to stay atop the NFC East. A highlight was a 59-yard TD strike from **Dak Prescott** to Tavon Austin.

✱ New TD King: **Drew Brees** floated a 5-yard TD pass to tight end **Josh Hill** as the Saints romped over the Colts 34–7. It was more than just six points, however. The pass was touchdown No. 540 in Brees' amazing career, making him the all-time career leader in scoring passes. He jumped over both **Peyton Manning** and **Tom Brady** in the game. He also set a single-game record with a 96.7 percent completion percentage!

✱ Record Streak: The Patriots beat the Bengals 34–13, which was not big news. What was big news was that the win sent New England to the playoffs for the 11th year in a row. In the 100 years of the NFL, no team had ever had a streak that long!

WEEK 16

✱ Move Over, Marvin: At the end of the Saints 38–28 win over the Titans, **Michael Thomas** had reached 145 catches for the season. That set a new NFL record, breaking the mark of **Marvin Harrison**, who had 143 in 2002. Thomas had 12 catches for New Orleans as they continued to try to clinch a first-round bye.

✱ Fly, Eagles, Fly!: With a half-dozen key players out because of injuries, the Eagles could have landed with a thud. Instead, they beat the Cowboys in Dallas 17–9. That put Philadelphia in first place in the NFC East. One more win and they would clinch a surprising playoff spot.

2019 Playoffs

WILD CARD WEEKEND

AFC: Titans 20, Patriots 13

Derrick Henry (182 rushing yards) and the Titans ran **Tom Brady** and the Patriots right out of the playoffs. Tennessee won in the Pats' home stadium!

AFC: Texans 22, Bills 19 (OT)

Down 16–0, Houston had a problem. But it also had the solution: QB **Deshaun Watson**. After the Bills owned the first half and shut out the Texans, Watson had a great second half. He led to them on three scoring drives. In overtime, he was nearly sacked by two Bills players. Watson escaped and threw the long pass that set up the game-winning field goal.

Davante Adams

NFC: Vikings 26, Saints 20 (OT)

Minnesota sent another star quarterback home as the Vikings upset the Saints and **Drew Brees**. The Vikings jumped out to a 20-10 lead. Brees brought the Saints back to tie the game on a long field goal. In overtime, Minnesota got the ball and won on a TD catch by **Kyle Rudolph**.

NFC: Seahawks 17, Eagles 9

Seattle's defense swarmed over the Eagles, recording seven sacks. Seattle's **DK Metcalf** set a rookie record with 160 receiving yards.

DIVISIONAL PLAYOFFS

49ers 27, Vikings 10

The Niners defense dominated. They had six sacks, forced two turnovers, and allowed just 21 yards rushing! **Tevin Coleman** ran for two scores.

Packers 28, Seahawks 23

Russell Wilson just ran out of time. Seattle's great comeback QB couldn't come up with the final score and Green Bay hung on to win. WR **Davante Adams** had eight catches for 160 yards and two scores to lead the Pack.

Titans 28, Ravens 12

No. 1 no more! The Titans shocked the top-seeded Ravens by shutting down **Lamar Jackson**. Henry starred again, piling up

195 yards rushing. Tennessee's defense forced two key turnovers and had two fourth-down stops that led to points.

Chiefs 51, Texans 31

The Chiefs fell behind 24–0 in the first quarter. By the end of the second, they led 28–24. No team in NFL history, regular or postseason, had ever done that! A big reason was the 4 TD passes by **Patrick Mahomes** in the second quarter, three to TE **Travis Kelce**.

AFC CONFERENCE CHAMPIONSHIP
Chiefs 35, Titans 24

Like they did against the Texans, the Chiefs fell behind early. Like they did against the Texans, they stormed back to win. Mahomes was a genius again. He threw three TD passes, including a 60-yard bomb to **Sammy Watkins**. Mahomes also created an instant highlight with a twisting, turning, tackle-avoiding 27-yard TD run. The Chiefs will play in their first Super Bowl in 50 years!

NFC CONFERENCE CHAMPIONSHIP
49ers 37, Packers 20

Green Bay didn't know what hit them. By the time the first half ended, the Niners were up 27–0

before cruising to a huge win. **Raheem Mostert** did the most damage. He became the first player in NFL history with 200 yards (he had 220) and 4 TDs in a postseason game. San Francisco's defense picked off two **Aaron Rodgers** passes, recovered a fumble, and recorded three sacks. The Niners will aim for their sixth Super Bowl championship!

Mostert ran wild against Green Bay.

Super Bowl LIV

The Chiefs trailed the Texans 24–0 and came back to win. They were behind the Titans 10–0 and won. So in Super Bowl LIV, when Kansas City was behind San Francisco 20–10 in the fourth quarter, the Chiefs had the Niners right where they wanted them!

With yet another **Patrick Mahomes**-led comeback, the Chiefs won their first Super Bowl in 50 years, 31–20. One huge play in the fourth quarter showed just how explosive the Chiefs

could be. Trailing by 10 and on a third-and-15, Mahomes connected on a 44-yard play to Tyreek Hill. KC scored soon after and the comeback trail was clear.

Up to that point, San Francisco looked dominant for most of the first three quarters-plus. Mahomes mostly bottled up, though he did score on a 1-yard run. The Niners tied the score 10–10 on a 15-yard TD catch by fullback

Williams scored his second TD late to ice the game for the Chiefs.

SUPER BOWL LIV

TEAM	1Q	2Q	3Q	4Q	FINAL
SAN FRANCISCO	3	7	10	0	20
KANSAS CITY	7	3	0	21	31

SCORING

Niners: FG Gould, 38
Chiefs: TD Mahomes 1 yd run (Butker kick)
Chiefs: FG Butker 31
Niners: TD Juszcyzk 15 pass from Garoppolo (Butker kick)
Niners: FG Gould 42
Niners: TD Mostert 1 run (Gould kick)
Chiefs: TD Kelce 1 pass from Mahomes (Butker kick)
Chiefs: TD D. Williams 5 pass from Mahomes (Butker kick)
Chiefs: TD D. Williams 38 run (Butker kick)

As in most things, it's not how you start, it's how you finish. The Niners let the Chiefs score the last three TDs of the game. It was "not again!" for SF coach **Kyle Shanahan.** He had been the offensive coordinator for Atlanta three seasons ago. His Falcons let the Patriots complete a record-breaking 25-point comeback.

Mahomes became the second-youngest QB to win a Super Bowl and the youngest to be named MVP!

Kyle Juszczyk. That was the halftime score, but it felt like the Niners were winning.

In the third quarter, the feeling became reality. The 49ers scored on the second half's opening drive. Mahomes then threw an interception and the Niners scored again, on a short, tough TD run by **Raheem Mostert,** to give the Niners a ten-point cushion. It was not enough.

The Hill catch led to a short TD catch by TE **Travis Kelce.** Then the Chiefs defense rose up and stopped the Niners. With the ball in his hands, Mahomes was unstoppable. He hit **Sammy Watkins** with a big pass. **Damien Williams** then caught a short pass and sneaked into the corner of the end zone. Just like that, the Chiefs led. Williams made it official with a 38-yard TD run late in the game to make the final score 31-20.

Mahomes carried the Lombardi Trophy to KC!

2019 Stats Leaders

1,540 RUSHING YARDS
Derrick Henry, Titans

149 RECEPTIONS
1,725 RECEIVING YARDS
Michael Thomas, Saints

11 TD RECEPTIONS
Kenny Golladay, Lions

36 TD PASSES
Lamar Jackson, Ravens

5,109 PASSING YARDS
Jameis Winston, Buccaneers

147 POINTS / **34** FIELD GOALS
Harrison Butker, Chiefs

6 INTERCEPTIONS
Stephon Gilmore, Patriots
Anthony Harris, Vikings
Tre'Davious White, Bills

159 TACKLES
Bobby Wagner, Seahawks

19.5 SACKS
Shaquil Barrett,
Buccaneers

Thomas's 149 catches were a new NFL record.

NFL Awards

MOST VALUABLE PLAYER
QB LAMAR JACKSON
RAVENS

DEFENSIVE PLAYER OF THE YEAR
CB STEPHON GILMORE
PATRIOTS

OFFENSIVE ROOKIE OF THE YEAR
QB KYLER MURRAY
CARDINALS

DEFENSIVE ROOKIE OF THE YEAR
DE NICK BOSA
49ERS

COMEBACK PLAYER OF THE YEAR
QB RYAN TANNEHILL
TITANS

COACH OF THE YEAR
JOHN HARBAUGH
RAVENS

WALTER PAYTON NFL MAN OF THE YEAR
DL CALAIS CAMPBELL
JAGUARS

Kyler Murray

FANTASY STARS

How did your team do? If you had some of these players, you probably did well! Points are from NFL.com.

POS	PLAYER	FANTASY POINTS
RB	Christian McCaffrey ▶▶▶	471.20
QB	Lamar Jackson	415.68
WR	Michael Thomas	374.60
TE	Travis Kelce	254.30
K	Harrison Butker	153.00
DEF	Patriots	224.00

Even More!

The Hall of Fame created a special class in honor of the NFL's 100th anniversary. Along with the group of five players voted on by writers, the Hall added these 15 NFL legends

EAGLES RECEIVER **HAROLD CARMICHAEL**
BEARS TACKLE **JIMBO COVERT**
STEELERS COACH **BILL COWHER**
PACKERS SAFETY **BOBBY DILLON**
COWBOYS SAFETY **CLIFF HARRIS**
JETS TACKLE **WINSTON HILL**
COWBOYS COACH **JIMMY JOHNSON**
LIONS DEFENSIVE TACKLE **ALEX KARRAS**
NFL FILMS PRESIDENT **STEVE SABOL**
STEELERS SAFETY **DONNIE SHELL**
1922-1931 NFL TACKLE **DUKE SLATER**
BROWNS RECEIVER **MAC SPEEDIE**
BEARS LINEBACKER **ED SPRINKLE**
FORMER NFL COMMISSIONER **PAUL TAGLIABUE**
NFL EXECUTIVE **GEORGE YOUNG**

Carmichael earned four Pro Bowl spots.

2020 Hall of Fame

Steve Atwater was a hard-hitting safety for the Denver Broncos. He was in eight Pro Bowls in his 11 seasons. He helped Denver win Super Bowls XXXII and XXXIII.

Isaac Bruce is one of only five players with 1,000 catches (1,024), 15,000 yards (15,208) and 90 TDs (91). Bruce had a huge TD catch in the Rams Super Bowl XXXIV win. ▶

Steve Hutchinson blasted holes for 11 1,000-yard rushers, including two NFL rushing champs, in 12 seasons. The big guard started all 169 games he played in for the Seahawks, Vikings, and Titans.

◀ **Edgerrin James** was a pounding runner, mostly for the Colts, who led the NFL in rushing twice with two of his six 1,200-plus-yard seasons. He helped them reach the playoffs six times.

Troy Polamalu earned fame for his amazing play and awesome hair! The Steelers safety played in eight Pro Bowls and was the 2010 NFL Defensive Player of the Year.

For the Record

Super Bowl Winners

GAME	SEASON	WINNING TEAM	LOSING TEAM	SCORE	SITE
LIV	2019	**Kansas City**	San Francisco	**31–20**	Miami
LIII	2018	**New England**	L.A. Rams	**13–3**	Atlanta
LII	2017	**Philadelphia**	New England	**41–33**	Minneapolis
LI	2016	**New England**	Atlanta	**34–28** (OT)	Houston
L	2015	**Denver**	Carolina	**24–10**	Santa Clara
XLIX	2014	**New England**	Seattle	**28–24**	Glendale, AZ
XLVIII	2013	**Seattle**	Denver	**43–8**	E. Rutherford, NJ
XLVII	2012	**Baltimore**	San Francisco	**34–31**	New Orleans
XLVI	2011	**NY Giants**	New England	**21–17**	Indianapolis
XLV	2010	**Green Bay**	Pittsburgh	**31–25**	Arlington, TX
XLIV	2009	**New Orleans**	Indianapolis	**31–17**	Miami
XLIII	2008	**Pittsburgh**	Arizona	**27–23**	Tampa
XLII	2007	**NY Giants**	New England	**17–14**	Glendale, AZ
XLI	2006	**Indianapolis**	Chicago	**29–17**	Miami
XL	2005	**Pittsburgh**	Seattle	**21–10**	Detroit
XXXIX	2004	**New England**	Philadelphia	**24–21**	Jacksonville
XXXVIII	2003	**New England**	Carolina	**32–29**	Houston
XXXVII	2002	**Tampa Bay**	Oakland	**48–21**	San Diego
XXXVI	2001	**New England**	St. Louis	**20–17**	New Orleans
XXXV	2000	**Baltimore**	NY Giants	**34–7**	Tampa
XXXIV	1999	**St. Louis**	Tennessee	**23–16**	Atlanta
XXXIII	1998	**Denver**	Atlanta	**34–19**	Miami
XXXII	1997	**Denver**	Green Bay	**31–24**	San Diego
XXXI	1996	**Green Bay**	New England	**35–21**	New Orleans
XXX	1995	**Dallas**	Pittsburgh	**27–17**	Tempe

GAME	SEASON	WINNING TEAM	LOSING TEAM	SCORE	SITE
XXIX	1994	San Francisco	San Diego	49–26	Miami
XXVIII	1993	Dallas	Buffalo	30–13	Atlanta
XXVII	1992	Dallas	Buffalo	52–17	Pasadena
XXVI	1991	Washington	Buffalo	37–24	Minneapolis
XXV	1990	NY Giants	Buffalo	20–19	Tampa
XXIV	1989	San Francisco	Denver	55–10	New Orleans
XXIII	1988	San Francisco	Cincinnati	20–16	Miami
XXII	1987	Washington	Denver	42–10	San Diego
XXI	1986	NY Giants	Denver	39–20	Pasadena
XX	1985	Chicago	New England	46–10	New Orleans
XIX	1984	San Francisco	Miami	38–16	Stanford
XVIII	1983	LA Raiders	Washington	38–9	Tampa
XVII	1982	Washington	Miami	27–17	Pasadena
XVI	1981	San Francisco	Cincinnati	26–21	Pontiac, MI
XV	1980	Oakland	Philadelphia	27–10	New Orleans
XIV	1979	Pittsburgh	Los Angeles	31–19	Pasadena
XIII	1978	Pittsburgh	Dallas	35–31	Miami
XII	1977	Dallas	Denver	27–10	New Orleans
XI	1976	Oakland	Minnesota	32–14	Pasadena
X	1975	Pittsburgh	Dallas	21–17	Miami
IX	1974	Pittsburgh	Minnesota	16–6	New Orleans
VIII	1973	Miami	Minnesota	24–7	Houston
VII	1972	Miami	Washington	14–7	Los Angeles
VI	1971	Dallas	Miami	24–3	New Orleans
V	1970	Baltimore	Dallas	16–13	Miami
IV	1969	Kansas City	Minnesota	23–7	New Orleans
III	1968	NY Jets	Baltimore	16–7	Miami
II	1967	Green Bay	Oakland	33–14	Miami
I	1966	Green Bay	Kansas City	35–10	Los Angeles
II	1967	Green Bay	Oakland	33–14	Miami

HUT, HUT, HIKE!

LSU's Joe Burrow gets the snap to start a play against Clemson in the College Football Playoff. The game capped off a great season on the gridiron. Read on to see more unique views and awesome facts and stats.

20

COLLEGE FOOTBALL

New Faces on Top!

College football was starting to be a copycat. The same two teams had traded off national titles every season since 2014. So it was big news when a new team jumped into the picture for the final trophy. The LSU Tigers put together one of the best seasons in college football history and captured the national championship.

Clemson and Alabama didn't disappear, however. Those were the two teams that had been regulars in the championship game. Clemson was once again in the picture, and made it to the final. Alabama, however, lost a big game to Auburn in November and didn't even make the final four. In fact, the Crimson Tide fell to No. 8, its lowest ranking since 2010.

Other teams arose to join the chase to the top of the rankings. Georgia made a great run, but a shocking loss to South Carolina put them in a hole. Oregon had its eye on the national playoffs, even after an opening loss to Auburn. They won nine in a row, but a loss to Arizona State ended their title hopes. Minnesota had one of its best seasons ever. It was 9-0 when it was upset by Iowa. Still, the Golden Gophers'

No. 10 ranking was its best since 1962!

Along with LSU and Clemson, Ohio State also looked like an early challenger for the top. Its offense seemed unstoppable. The Buckeyes scored 45 or more points in eight wins, including a stunning 73–14 win over Maryland. QB **Justin Fields** passed for 41 touchdowns!

Oklahoma was the fourth team in the final four. The Sooners were led by former Alabama QB **Jalen Hurts**. They put on an offensive show, topping 40 points in eight of its wins. They met their match against LSU, however, in the national semifinal.

LSU was THE huge story of the season. They just kept getting better and better, piling up points in record amounts. They had eight 50-point games on the way to setting a Football Bowl Division record with 726 points. They were the first SEC team ever to go 15–0. **Joe Burrow** was the easy Heisman winner and his 61 total TD passes were an all-time record.

No more copycats. LSU stands alone, roaring as the 2019 national champs!

Jalen Hurts

FINAL TOP 10

1. LSU
2. Clemson
3. Ohio State
4. Georgia
5. Oregon
6. Florida
7. Oklahoma
8. Alabama
9. Penn State
10. Minnesota

AWARDS

HEISMAN TROPHY (BEST OVERALL PLAYER)
MAXWELL AWARD (TOP ALL-AROUND PLAYER)
WALTER CAMP AWARD (TOP PLAYER)
DAVEY O'BRIEN TROPHY (TOP QB)
Joe Burrow/LSU (RIGHT)

DOAK WALKER AWARD (RUNNING BACK)
Jonathan Taylor/WISCONSIN

FRED BILETNIKOFF AWARD (RECEIVER)
Ja'Marr Chase/LSU

BEDNARIK AWARD (DEFENSE)
NAGURSKI TROPHY (DEFENSE)
Chase Young/OHIO STATE

OUTLAND TROPHY (LINEMAN)
Penei Sewell/OREGON

JIM THORPE AWARD (DB)
Grant Delpit/LSU

LOU GROZA AWARD (KICKER)
Rodrigo Blankenship/GEORGIA

COACH OF THE YEAR
Ed Orgeron/LSU

August/September
SEASON HIGHLIGHTS

➔ **Opening Upset:** Tennessee didn't "volunteer" for this bit of news. (Get it? Tennessee's nickname is the Volunteers!) Georgia State was a 25-point underdog in the teams' opening-weekend game. The underdog barked last, as GSU pulled off a stunning upset, 38–30. GSU had been on a seven-game losing streak and had never beaten a team from the SEC before!

➔ **Aloha to a W:** The defense for Arizona must not have made the airplane trip to Hawaii. Then again, the Rainbows' D took the day off, too. The two teams combined for 1,134 total yards. Hawaii was often ahead, but Arizona repeatedly came back. The Wildcats had a chance to tie, but the Hawaii defense showed up at the right moment for a game-saving goal-line stop for the 45–38 win.

➔ **Big Early Win:** LSU jumped into the top four in the country after a big win over No. 9 Texas, 45–38. LSU's **Joe Burrow** had 4 TD passes and threw for 471 yards. The battle between top-10 teams featured a lot of scoring. The Longhorns made it close with a late TD, but the Tigers held on.

➔ **Make a Kick, Win Free College:** Nevada roared back to tie Purdue at 31–31 after trailing 24–7 at one point in their season-opening game. In overtime, Wolf Pack kicker **Brandon Talton** kicked an incredible 56-yard field goal for the winning points. After the celebration, his coach told him that the school had awarded him a full scholarship to keep kicking (and studying, of course). Time for another celebration!

➔ **100 and a TO:** Two great Pennsylvania schools played their 100th game against each other, but it will be the last for some time. No. 13 Penn State beat Pitt 17–10. That gave them a 53–43–4 record in the series,

WSU's Anthony Gordon

which began in 1893, but is not scheduled again for several years.

➡ 100 and a TO: Two great

Pennsylvania schools played their 100th game against each other, but it will be the last for some time. No. 13 Penn State beat Pitt 17–10. That gave PSU a 53-43-4 record in the series, which began in 1893, but is not scheduled again for several years.

➡ Hubba Hubbard!: Oklahoma State's

awesomely named **Chuba Hubbard** had his second straight 200-yard game, running for 256 yards as the Cowboys beat Tulsa 40-21. His big play was a 75-yard run for a score on the game's first play!

➡ What a Comeback!: UCLA

trailed Washington State in the third quarter by an incredible 32 points. The Bruins' defense was giving up yards in huge bunches and the offense struggled. Still, UCLA kept fighting... and scoring. The two teams combined for 43 points in the fourth quarter alone! At the end, UCLA was on top 67-63–it was the highest scoring game in Pac-12 history! Washington State's **Anthony Gordon** set his own conference mark record with 9 TD passes on the loss.

➡ Streak Ends: No. 15 Central Florida

had won 27 regular-season games in a row, dating back to 2016, but the streak ended at Pittsburgh. The Panthers scored on a trick play,

A Taylor TD helped Wisconsin win.

as QB **Kenny Pickett** caught a TD pass, and Pitt won 35–34.

➡ Big Ten Battle: No. 13 Wisconsin

manhandled No. 11 Michigan 35–14. The Wolverines' star running back, **Jonathan Taylor**, scored twice and rumbled for 203 yards on the ground.

➡ Tar Heels Get Stuck: North

Carolina had a chance for a big upset against No. 1 Clemson. After scoring late in the game, the Heels decided to go for two points and the win rather than kick a tying PAT. Clemson stuffed the run attempt and escaped with a close 21–20 win.

October
SEASON HIGHLIGHTS

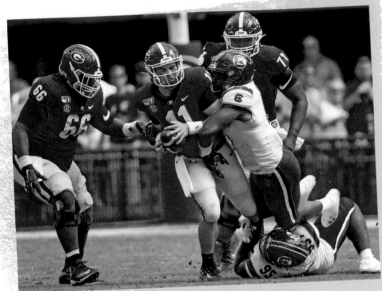

South Carolina upset Georgia!

→ **Go, Go, Gators:** No. 10 Florida remained unbeaten while handing No. 7 Auburn its first loss of the season. An 88-yard run by **Lamical Perine** helped the Gators beat the Tigers 24–13.

→ **D-Fense! D-Fense!:** Michigan sacked the Iowa QB eight times. The Wolverines took advantage of four Hawkeyes turnovers, too, and won a key Big 10 game 10–3.

→ **SEC Upset:** Unranked South Carolina pulled off the biggest upset of 2019 (so far!) with a two-overtime win over No. 3 Georgia. The Bulldogs committed four turnovers, handing the Gamecocks good field position. A possible game-tying field goal for Georgia was just wide.

→ **Tigers Roar:** Unbeaten LSU jumped to No. 2 overall after beating No. 7 Florida 42–28. QB **Joe Burrow** continued his hot play with three TD passes in leading LSU to a comeback win.

→ **Football Game or Dance Show?:** Between the third and fourth quarters, Georgia Southern and Coastal Carolina, for some reason, held a "dance-off" on the field. Most of both teams came off the benches to do the "Mo Bamba." The refs were not happy! When the dancing was over, the game was entertaining, too! Tied 10–10, the game didn't end until after the third overtime. **Wesley Kennedy II** ran in a TD for GSU to clinch the win.

→ **Turnover Trouble:** Coaches will tell you nothing is more important than holding onto the ball! Memphis lost a chance at an unbeaten season by not listening. They had four turnovers in the game, including three in the first half. They had a chance to win late, but a catch was overturned by replay. Temple held on for a surprising 30–28 win.

→ **Red River Rivalry:** The annual Oklahoma vs Texas battle takes its name from the river that separates the two states. Only seven points separated the two teams after a hard-fought game, as No. 6 OU remained unbeaten, beating No. 11 UT 34–27. Former Alabama star **Jalen Hurts** had 3 TD passes for the Sooners.

→ **Down Go the Badgers: James McCourt** enjoyed a ride off the field on his fellow Illinois students' shoulder. He had just kicked a 39-yard field goal on the final play. That gave Illinois a shocking 24–23 upset over No. 6 Wisconsin. The home team had been 30.5 point underdogs!

→ **Cool Casey:** Minnesota player **Casey O'Brien** was the hero of his team's 42–7 over Rutgers even though all he did was hold for extra points. Why the fuss? O'Brien has survived FOUR bouts with cancer and battled to get back in shape to play his favorite sport. His coach was in tears after the game talking about O'Brien as an inspiration. Impressive!

→ **Pac-12 Streaks End:** Arizona State was held to fewer than 10 points for the first time after matching the all-time record of 125 games! Utah's defense shut down the Sun Devils 21–3 for a big win. UCLA ended another streak by beating Stanford 34–16. The Bruins had lost 11 straight to the Cardinal!

→ **October Surprise:** The final weekend of October (a few days before Halloween!) produced some scary surprises in the Top 10. Kansas State shocked No. 5 Oklahoma as QB **Skylar Thompson** ran for four TDs in his team's 48–41 win. No. 8 Notre Dame was washed out 45–14 in a rain-soaked upset by Michigan. No. 9 Auburn lost, but at least they fell to a higher-ranked team, No. 2 LSU. With the 23–20 win, LSU jumped over Alabama as the new No. 1 team.

Illinois K James McCourt was a Badger-killer!

November
SEASON HIGHLIGHTS

➔ **Busy Day:** Memphis receiver **Antonio Gibson** was pretty tired after his team's win over SMU. No surprise there. He caught a 50-yard TD pass, ran 78 yards for another score, and returned a kickoff 97 yards for a third! His play was a big reason that the Tigers beat undefeated SMU 54–48 in an exciting shootout.

➔ **Bulldogs Are Back:** Georgia kept its national playoff hopes alive with a big win over No. 6 Florida. A 52-yard TD pass from

Chase Garbers led Cal to a "Big" win.

Jake Fromm to **Lawrence Cager** was a key score, but Florida came back twice. Fromm iced the game with a late third-down pass to complete the 24–17 win.

➔ **SEC Showdown:** One national poll put Alabama No. 1. The College Football Playoff (CFP) poll had LSU No. 1. The two top-ranked teams met in a huge November battle and LSU ended up on top. The Tigers won 46–41, beating the Tide for the first time since 2011. QB **Joe Burrow** led the way with 3 TD passes. Alabama made it close, scoring with just over a minute left. However, LSU recovered the onside kick and closed out the huge win.

➔ **Go, Go, Gophers!:** Minnesota's Golden Gophers moved to 9–0 for the first time in 115 years! They had to defeat unbeaten No. 4 Penn State to do so. An end-zone interception by **Jordan Howden** sealed the 31–26 upset victory that scrambled the CFP rankings.

➔ **Bye-Bye, Gophers!:** Minnesota's dream season hit a huge roadblock in Iowa. The Hawkeyes upset the No. 7 Gophers 23–19. It was the first loss of the year for Minnesota, but it was the school's ninth in a row at Iowa.

➔ **What a Comeback!:** Kent State trailed Buffalo 27–6 with eight minutes left. Guess

Gibson led the way for Memphis.

who won? The Golden Flash put together a game-ending series of plays that shocked everyone watching. First, they scored and recovered an onside kick. They scored again to get closer. Buffalo had to punt, but Kent State blocked it and recovered for a game-tying TD! After another Buffalo punt, Kent State's **Matthew Trickett** kicked a game-winning 44-yard field goal.

→ **Sooners Return?:** Oklahoma bounced back from a loss to Kansas State a few weeks earlier to beat undefeated No. 13 Baylor 34–31. **Jalen Hurts** threw 4 TDs for the Sooners, but it was a late field goal by **Gabe Brkic** that gave them the winning points. OU trailed by 21 points at halftime, but the defense showed up in the second half, holding Baylor scoreless.

→ **Oh, No, Oregon!:** The No. 6 Ducks were on their way to a Pac-12 showdown with No. 7 Utah. The winner of their struggle probably had a shot at the College Football Playoff. Oregon ruined that chance when it lost to Arizona State 31–28. The Sun Devils picked off two Oregon passes late to seal the upset.

→ **Don't Leave Early:** Anyone who gave up their seat in the fourth quarter of the Washington State-Oregon State game made a big mistake. The Cougars took a 43–32 lead only to watch the Beavers chew their way back thanks to an onside kick and an interception. WSU scored to get close and then with just two seconds left, **Max Borghi** dove into the end zone for the wild 54–53 win.

→ **Finally!:** California beat archrival Stanford 24–20 in The Big Game. Why is that news? It was the first win for the Golden Bears after nine straight losses to the Cardinal. The two schools' big rivalry dates back to 1892.

→ **Iron Bowl Classic:** Alabama expected to win the annual Iron Bowl rivalry with Auburn and set itself up for another College Football Playoff spot. The Tigers made sure that didn't happen. **Anders Carlson** made four field goals and the Auburn D returned two picks for six (including one for 100 yards!). The Tigers held on for a 48–45 win over a surprised Crimson Tide.

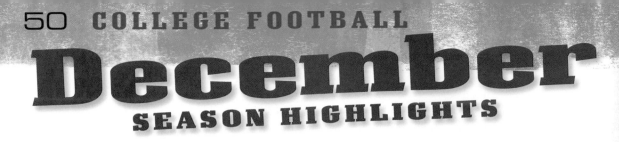

December
SEASON HIGHLIGHTS

CONFERENCE CHAMPIONSHIPS

AAC MEMPHIS 29
CINCINNATI 24

The third time was the charm for the Tigers. A TD pass from **Brady White** to **Antonio Gibson** put them ahead to stay with just over a minute remaining. It was another big day for RB Gibson, who also had a 65-yard TD run. Memphis also got help from kicker **Riley Patterson**, who made field goals of 50 and 52 yards.

CJ Verdell and the Ducks quacked last.

ACC CLEMSON 62
VIRGINIA 17

It was the T. and Tee show as Clemson cemented its spot in the Playoff again. QB **Trevor Lawrence** connected with WR **Tee Higgins** on 3 TD passes as the Tigers romped. Lawrence's total of 4 TD passes was an ACC title game record. Higgins earned his own place in the books with 182 receiving yards.

Big Ten OHIO STATE 34
WISCONSIN 21

For a while, it looked like the Badgers would pull off the upset and mix up the Playoff possibilities. Then the Buckeyes' powerful offense responded. Trailing 21–7 at halftime, Ohio State roared back, scoring 27 unanswered points. QB **Justin Fields** had three TD passes, while RB **J.K. Dobbins** ran for 172 yards.

Big 12 OKLAHOMA 30
BAYLOR 23 (OT)

Oklahoma had a wide-open path to the Playoff after Utah lost. Then Baylor tried to spoil the Sooners' party. The Bears' freshman QB **Jacob Zeno** helped his team tie the favored Sooners late in the game. In overtime, OU RB **Rhamondre Stevenson** rambled five yards for the winning score. It was Oklahoma's fifth straight Big 12 title.

Mountain West BOISE STATE 31
HAWAII 10

It's not how you start, it's how you finish. **Jaylon Henderson** started 2019 as the backup for the Broncos. Thanks to an injury to the starter, he ended it as the championship-

Justin Field and Ohio State rumbled over Wisconsin to win the Big Ten title.

game MVP after throwing two TD passes. The Boise defense came up big. Twice they stopped Hawaii on fourth down inside the 5-yard line.

Pac-12 OREGON 37 UTAH 15

The Utes needed one more win to earn a spot in the College Football Playoff. Just seven minutes into the game, that spot had disappeared. The Ducks rolled to a 20–0 lead before halftime, and capped off their conference title with two long TD runs by **CJ Verdell**.

SEC LSU 37 GEORGIA 10

Did LSU QB **Joe Burrow** lock up the Heisman Trophy? He sure looked like college football's best in leading his team to the SEC title. The first of Burrow's 4 TD passes also made him the all-time SEC single-season record-holder with 45. Burrow also ran for 41 yards and even caught a deflected pass! The Tigers earned the Playoff No. 1 seed in large part thanks to their star passer.

Sun Belt APPALACHIAN STATE 45 LOUISIANA-LAFAYETTE 38

This was a rematch of the teams' regular-season game. The score was a bit different, though. In the first, ASU won a defensive struggle 17–7. The conference championship game was a scoreboard-buster. ASU piled up 416 yards of offense. RB Darrynton Evans was the workhorse. He scored 89 yards and 3 TDs. ASU ended the season at 13–1 and was ranked No. 19, its highest mark ever.

2019 Bowl Bonanza!

The 2019 season included 40 bowl games. Here are some of the most memorable moments outside of the College Football Playoff semifinals and national championship.

ONE IF BY AIR: The US Navy usually wins battles with ships. In the 2019 Liberty Bowl, the Navy football team won through the air! On a fourth down late in the game, Navy used a trick play—a pass by running back **CJ Williams**—to set up a field goal. With two seconds left, **Bijan Nichols** made the kick and Navy beat Kansas State 20–17.

Win the Potato Bowl and you get fries!

GOOD TIMING!: The San Diego State Aztecs saved their best for last. In the New Mexico Bowl, they walloped Central Michigan 48–11. It was the most points SDSU had scored in a game in more than two seasons! They had not even reached 26 points since a game in September 2019. They saved the big points for the big game!

DUCKS QUACK BACK: In the Rose Bowl, Oregon looked like it was going down to defeat against Wisconsin. In the fourth quarter, though, the Ducks quacked! They forced a key fumble. **Justin Herbert** soon ran in for a touchdown to take the lead. Oregon held on to win 28–27. Wisconsin gained more yards and had the ball for more than 38 of the game's 60 minutes, but its four turnovers were the difference.

UNUSUAL DUNKS: You've seen coaches splashed with water and sports drinks after games. This bowl season saw some very odd late-game dunkings. At the Tropical Smoothie Bowl, Kent State coach **Sean Lewis** got splashed with a giant green kale smoothie. Air Force dropped cheese crackers over its coach after a win in the (you guessed it!) Cheez-It Bowl. It was clearly a trend. Players from Arizona State dumped Frosted Flakes on the coach after the Tony the Tiger Sun Bowl. In Boise, the winning coach in the Famous Idaho Potato Bowl, Ohio's **Frank Solich**, was covered in french fries! Good thing there is not a Chili Bowl!

MORE THAN JUST THE BIG GUYS

College football includes more than 775 teams on five levels. The College Football Playoff gets the big headlines for the Football Bowl Series (FBS), but let's give these other champs their due.

FCS North Dakota State used a touchdown on a fake field goal to help defeat **James Madison** 28–20. It was NDSU's eighth title at this level (which used to be called 1-AA), all within the past nine seasons! They also became the first team since Yale way back in 1894 to go 16–0 over a full season.

Div. II It only took 30 minutes for West Florida's **Austin Reed** (right) to set a championship-game record with 399 passing yards. He wound up with 523, and he'd need every one. His team held off Minnesota State 48–40 for the title. Reed had six passing TDs, three to **Quentin Randolph**. West Florida had to hold off MSU in the final minute to save the win.

Div. III The running game carried North Central (Ill.) to a huge 41–14 win over Wisconsin-Whitewater. **Ethan Greenfield** (below) had 138 rushing yards and three TDs.

NAIA Morningside held on for a 40–38 win over Marian University to earn its second straight title in this division of smaller schools. Both teams entered the game undefeated, so it was no surprise the score was so close. QB **Joe Dolincheck** was the big story, throwing six TD passes for Morningside.

College Football Playoff

National Semifinals

LSU 63, Oklahoma 28

Lucky seven! That's how many TD passes LSU star **Joe Burrow** threw in this rout. He tied an all-time, all-bowl record . . . and the scoring strikes all came in the first half! **Justin Jefferson** caught four of them. That also tied a bowl-game record. LSU scored the first time it had the ball and never looked back. Burrow even ran for a score in the second half!

Clemson 29, Ohio State 23

Clemson trailed OSU 16–0 but then **Trevor Lawrence** took over. The Clemson QB, who had never lost a college game, ran 67 yards for a key score. It was 16–14 OSU at halftime. Lawrence threw two TD passes to **Travis Etienne** in the second half, one of them for 53 yards. The last score came with less than two minutes left. Clemson then picked off an OSU pass in the end zone to seal the clutch victory.

Lawrence's 67-yard TD run helped the Clemson Tigers rally to beat Ohio State.

National Championship

If two tigers fought, who would win? That's how the 2019 College Football Championship was decided: The LSU Tigers vs. the Clemson Tigers. In the early going, Clemson's Tigers looked like they would roar the loudest. Star QB **Trevor Lawrence** led the defending champions. He ran for a score and when wide receiver **Tee Higgins** scored on a reverse, it gave Clemson an early 17-7 lead.

But LSU's own superstar QB took over. Heisman Trophy winner **Joe Burrow**, who had dropped a perfect 52-yard pass into the hands of a speeding **Ja'Marr Chase** for LSU's first touchdown, was ready to do some roaring of his own. In the second quarter, Burrow ran in for another score and then proceeded to rewrite the record books.

The cool and calm passer added two more TD passes in the second quarter. LSU led at halftime 28–17, but it wasn't that close.

Still, Clemson kept clawing back. They got to within three points at 28–25 on a run by **Travis Etienne**.

Burrow put the pedal to the metal. Two more TD passes put the game on ice en route to a 42-25 victory. Burrow's five TDs and 463 passing yards were a record for championship games in the FBS era. Also, his fourth TD in the game (to tight end **Thaddeus Moss**, whose dad is Hall of Fame receiver **Randy Moss**!) gave him 59 overall for the season. That also set a new single-season NCAA record. He ended up with 60. Add in Burrow's five total rushing TDs on the year and he was responsible for 65 scores, another record.

LSU became just the second team to go 15–0 in more than 100 years. The other one—last year's Clemson team!

Terrace Marshall's TD capped the scoring

We're No. 1!

These are the teams that have finished at the top of the Associated Press's final rankings since the poll was first introduced in 1936.

SEASON	TEAM	RECORD	SEASON	TEAM	RECORD
2019	LSU	15–0	1977	Notre Dame	11–1
2018	Clemson	15–0	1976	Pittsburgh	12–0
2017	Alabama	13–1	1975	Oklahoma	11–1
2016	Clemson	14–1	1974	Oklahoma	11–0
2015	Alabama	14–1	1973	Notre Dame	11–0
2014	Ohio State	14–1	1972	USC	12–0
2013	Florida State	14–0	1971	Nebraska	13–0
2012	Alabama	13–1	1970	Nebraska	11–0–1
2011	Alabama	12–1	1969	Texas	11–0
2010	Auburn	14–0	1968	Ohio State	10–0
2009	Alabama	14–0	1967	USC	10–1
2008	Florida	13–1	1966	Notre Dame	9–0–1
2007	LSU	12–2	1965	Alabama	9–1–1
2006	Florida	13–1	1964	Alabama	10–1
2005	Texas	13–0	1963	Texas	11–0
2004	USC	13–0	1962	USC	11–0
2003	USC	12–1	1961	Alabama	11–0
2002	Ohio State	14–0	1960	Minnesota	8–2
2001	Miami (FL)	12–0	1959	Syracuse	11–0
2000	Oklahoma	13–0	1958	LSU	11–0
1999	Florida State	12–0	1957	Auburn	10–0
1998	Tennessee	13–0	1956	Oklahoma	10–0
1997	Michigan	12–0	1955	Oklahoma	11–0
1996	Florida	12–1	1954	Ohio State	10–0
1995	Nebraska	12–0	1953	Maryland	10–1
1994	Nebraska	13–0	1952	Michigan State	9–0
1993	Florida State	12–1	1951	Tennessee	10–1
1992	Alabama	13–0	1950	Oklahoma	10–1
1991	Miami (FL)	12–0	1949	Notre Dame	10–0
1990	Colorado	11–1–1	1948	Michigan	9–0
1989	Miami (FL)	11–1	1947	Notre Dame	9–0
1988	Notre Dame	12–0	1946	Notre Dame	8–0–1
1987	Miami (FL)	12–0	1945	Army	9–0
1986	Penn State	12–0	1944	Army	9–0
1985	Oklahoma	11–1	1943	Notre Dame	9–1
1984	Brigham Young	13–0	1942	Ohio State	9–1
1983	Miami (FL)	11–1	1941	Minnesota	8–0
1982	Penn State	11–1	1940	Minnesota	8–0
1981	Clemson	12–0	1939	Texas A&M	11–0
1980	Georgia	12–0	1938	Texas Christian	11–0
1979	Alabama	12–0	1937	Pittsburgh	9–0–1
1978	Alabama	11–1	1936	Minnesota	7–1

NATIONAL CHAMPIONSHIP GAMES

Until the 2014 season, there was no national championship playoff system at the highest level of college football. From 1998 to 2013, the NCAA ran the Bowl Championship Series, which used computers and polls to come up with a final game that pitted the No. 1 team against the No. 2 team. The new system, called the College Football Playoff, has a panel of experts that sets up a pair of semifinal games to determine which teams play for the national title. Here are the results of BCS and College Football Playoff finals since 2000.

SEASON	TEAMS AND SCORE	SITE
2019	**LSU 42, Clemson 25**	NEW ORLEANS, LA
2018	**Clemson 44, Alabama 16**	SANTA CLARA, CA
2017	**Alabama 26, Georgia 20** (OT)	NEW ORLEANS, LA
2016	**Clemson 35, Alabama 31**	TAMPA, FL
2015	**Alabama 45, Clemson 40**	GLENDALE, AZ
2014	**Ohio State 42, Oregon 20**	ARLINGTON, TX
2013	**Florida State 34, Auburn 31**	PASADENA, CA
2012	**Alabama 42, Notre Dame 14**	MIAMI, FL
2011	**Alabama 21, LSU 0**	NEW ORLEANS, LA
2010	**Auburn 22, Oregon 19**	GLENDALE, AZ
2009	**Alabama 37, Texas 21**	PASADENA, CA
2008	**Florida 24, Oklahoma 14**	MIAMI, FL
2007	**LSU 38, Ohio State 24**	NEW ORLEANS, LA
2006	**Florida 41, Ohio State 14**	GLENDALE, AZ
2005	**Texas 41, USC 38**	PASADENA, CA
2004	**USC 55, Oklahoma 19**	MIAMI, FL
2003	**LSU 21, Oklahoma 14**	NEW ORLEANS, LA
2002	**Ohio State 31, Miami (FL) 24** (2 OT)	TEMPE, AZ
2001	**Miami (FL) 37, Nebraska 14**	PASADENA, CA
2000	**Oklahoma 13, Florida State 2**	MIAMI, FL

NATS WIN!

The Washington Nationals surprised almost everyone except themselves by beating the Houston Astros to win the 2019 World Series. It was the first championship in Nationals history! Washington's players were the oldest (by average) in the league, but they showed the kids a thing or two. The Nationals won in seven exciting games. Read all about it and more news of the 2019 and 2020 seasons inside!

The "Nationals" Pastime

Baseball has a famous nickname in the US: The National Pastime. While it's no longer the most popular sport (take one good guess what is), baseball has been a big part of America since the 1850s. The nation's capital has seen a lot of baseball during that time, but people there had not celebrated a championship since way back in 1933, when the Washington Senators won the World Series. That all changed in 2019 when the Washington Nationals earned their team's first World Series title.

When the playoffs began, though, that was certainly not what most fans expected. Several "super-teams" had better records, bigger stars, and more power. Washington just found a way to keep winning.

NL MVP Cody Bellinger

2019 FINAL MLB STANDINGS

AL EAST		AL CENTRAL		AL WEST	
Yankees	103–59	Twins	101–61	Astros	107–55
Rays	96–66	Indians	93–69	Athletics	97–65
Red Sox	84–78	White Sox	72–89	Rangers	78–84
Blue Jays	67–95	Royals	59–103	Angels	72–90
Orioles	54–108	Tigers	47–114	Mariners	68–94

NL EAST		NL CENTRAL		NL WEST	
Braves	97–65	Cardinals	91–71	Dodgers	106–56
Nationals	93–69	Brewers	89–73	Diamondbacks	85–77
Mets	86–76	Cubs	84–78	Giants	77–85
Phillies	81–81	Reds	75–87	Rockies	71–91
Marlins	57–105	Pirates	69–93	Padres	70–92

The Houston Astros had the best record in baseball, and put together perhaps the best 1-2-3 pitching punch ever. **Justin Verlander** won the Cy Young Award. **Gerrit Cole** came in second. **Zach Greinke** was a former Cy Young winner and won the Gold Glove. They won the AL title, but could not squeak by the surprising Nats.

The Dodgers were another one of those super-teams. But they probably wished the season ended before the playoffs. They had the best overall record in the NL and won the NL West for the seventh season in a row. Once again, though, they failed to win the championship. The team has a pile of stars and hit homers almost every game, but found ways to lose in the playoffs again.

The Yankees had the second most wins in the AL and were even bigger homer hitters than the Dodgers. Their big strength was their depth. New York lost a dozen top players to injuries at various times throughout the season. Still, they rallied until losing to the Astros in the ALCS.

The Red Sox were the powerhouse team of 2018, but the lights went out in 2019. Boston's hitters stopped bashing and their pitching flopped. Boston still has some great players, but couldn't find the magic they had in '18.

How do the Rays and Athletics do it? Are they using mirrors or magic tricks? Both teams are near the bottom of the list in player salaries. That is, they pay their players the least in the league—the Red Sox spent $151 million more than the Rays in 2019! But somehow, while Boston watched, Tampa Bay and Oakland both made the playoffs.

In the World Series, Washington proved to be kryptonite to Houston's super-team. Read on for more news about the 2019 season and the action-packed playoffs and World Series.

Austin Meadows

671

That is the difference between the old single-season home run record for MLB and the new one set in 2019. That's more than a ten percent increase!

Around the Bases 2019

Loud in London:
The Yankees and Red Sox played two regular-season games in London in June. They gave the Brits a real show! The two teams must have left their pitchers on the airplane. The hitters combined for 50 runs, 65 hits, and 10 homers in just two games! It was 6-6 after the first inning of the first matchup. New York won both, 17–13 and 12–8. Blimey!

Amazing Tribute:
The Angels lost a teammate when pitcher **Tyler Skaggs** died suddenly on July 1, 2019. The team and all of baseball was very sad. Then the Angels did something amazing. In their first home game after his death, every Angels player wore his No. 45 jersey. Incredibly, the team then threw a no-hitter! **Taylor Cole** opened with two perfect innings. **Felix Peña** came on and allowed no hits in his seven, allowing only one walk. Somewhere an Angel was smiling.

Family Ties:
Baseball has a long tradition of families. Dozens of MLB players have been related as father-son, brothers, or grandsons. In 2019, there were three great baseball family stories. First, Toronto 2B **Cavan Biggio** hit for the cycle on September 17. His father, Craig, had done the same for the Astros! On the same night, San Francisco OF **Mike Yastrzemski** hit a homer against the Boston Red Sox at Fenway Park. Mike's grandfather, **Carl**, was a Hall of Fame OF for the Bosox for 23 years! Earlier, Miami P **Brian Moran** struck out his brother, Pirates IF **Colin**!

No-No-No!:
Houston ace **Justin Verlander** became only the sixth pitcher ever with three career no-hitters. He held the Toronto Blue Jays hitless on September 1. Verlander had earlier no-nos with the Detroit Tigers in 2007 and 2011. It was part of a dream season for the Astros pitchers. **Gerrit Cole** and Verlander finished with the two best ERAs in the AL, and **Zack Greinke**, a midseason pickup, had the ninth-best ERA in MLB.

Justin Verlander: A triple no-hit pitcher

Classic Comeback:

On their way to earning an NL wild-card spot, the Washington Nationals had one of the season's most amazing comebacks. They trailed the Mets 10–4 entering the bottom of the ninth inning. Then the hit parade began. They put together six hits, including a walk-off homer by **Kurt Suzuki** to come back and win 11–10. Before that game, 2019 teams were 274–0 when leading by six in the ninth.

More Cool Stats:

In June, Colorado's **Charlie Blackmon** set a new record with 15 hits in a four-game series . . . The Astros were the first team since 2002 with a pair of 300-K pitchers— **Justin Verlander** and **Gerrit Cole**. . . . On the season's final day, both the Mets and Red Sox won on walk-off hits. The Mets' win came courtesy of **Dominic Smith's** homer, which was the 6,776th and last homer of the record-setting season.

Smith hit the last homer of a homer-happy year.

HOME RUN CRAZY!

If the 2019 season will be remembered for anything, it's for the incredible number of home runs that flew out of ballparks. Here are just a few of the new long-ball records set this season.

MOST HOME RUNS, ALL TEAMS: **6,776**

MOST HOME RUNS, SINGLE TEAM: **307**, MINNESOTA TWINS

MOST HOME RUNS, NL TEAM: **279**, LOS ANGELES DODGERS

MOST PLAYERS WITH 30-PLUS HOMERS: **58**

TEAMS THAT SET NEW ALL-TIME BESTS: **15**

MOST HOME RUNS ALLOWED: **305**, BALTIMORE ORIOLES

MOST PLAYERS WITH 30-PLUS HOMERS: **5**, MINNESOTA TWINS

MOST PLAYERS WITH 10-PLUS HOMERS: **14**, NY YANKEES

MOST HOME RUNS BY A ROOKIE: **53**, PETE ALONSO, NY METS

MLB Playoffs

Wild-Card Games

NL: Washington's **Juan Soto** knocked in two runs with a bases-loaded double in the bottom of the eighth. Another run scored when his hit got by the Milwaukee Brewers outfielder. The hit capped off a big comeback and Washington won 4–3.

AL: **Yandy Diaz** smacked two homers to lead the Tampa Bay Rays to a 5–1 win over the Oakland A's. Diaz was playing in just his second game since an injury back in July!

Torres went yard for the Bronx Bombers.

Division Series

ALDS

Yankees 3, Twins 0

The Bronx Bombers jumped all over the Twins, outscoring them 23–7 in a three-game sweep. 2B **Gleyber Torres** cracked his first postseason homer in Game 3, starting off a hot playoff run for the young star.

Astros 3, Rays 2

Tampa put a scare into Houston, which led MLB with 107 wins in 2019. After the Astros won the first two games, the Rays used great pitching and home-field fan power to even the series. Back in Houston, **Gerrit Cole's** 10 Ks in a win gave him a Division Series-record 25.

NLDS

Cardinals 3, Braves 2

The first four games of this series were great baseball, tight games with great action on both sides. The two teams split at each other's ballparks; after four games, the series was tied. St. Louis held off elimination thanks to a walk-off sacrifice fly by C **Yadier Molina** in Game 4. The drama of Game 5 vanished early. St. Louis scored a record 10 runs in the first inning on the way to a 13–1 victory.

Nationals 3, Dodgers 2

Washington crushed LA's hopes of a third straight NL title with a stunning grand slam by **Howie Kendrick** in the decisive Game 5. The teams traded wins to that point, with the Nationals getting to Dodgers ace **Clayton Kershaw** in Game 2. Kershaw also gave up back-to-back homers to set up Kendrick's big blow.

ALCS

Houston 4, Yankees 2

Walk-off! A tense series ended in Houston when 2B **José Altuve** smacked a series-winning walk-off homer in the bottom of the ninth of Game 6. The Astros thought they had the game wrapped up an inning earlier, but **D.J. LeMahieu** hit a game-tying two-run homer to set up ALCS MVP Altuve's heroics. Houston pitcher **Gerrit Cole** was outstanding again with a key Game 3 win. The Astros made it to their second World Series in three years; they won it all in 2017.

Kolten Wong scores a Cards' game-winner.

NLCS

Washington 4, St. Louis 0

The NLCS did not have nearly as much drama as the ALCS. Washington's power pitching told the whole story. In the first two games, **Anibal Sanchez** and **Max Scherzer** each had a no-hitter through six innings on the way to Nationals wins. In Game 3, **Stephen Strasburg** gave up 7 hits but no earned runs. After three games, Washington starters had a 0.00 ERA. 2B **Howie Kendrick** contributed four doubles and four RBI and was named the NLCS MVP. Washington earned its team's first World Series trip!

Rendon powered the Nationals to a surprising Series title.

2019 World Series

GAME 1: Nationals 5, Astros 4

Washington quieted Houston's loud fans by scoring five runs off pitcher **Gerrit Cole**, who had not lost a game since May! OF **Juan Soto** knocked in three runs for the Nats, while starter **Max Scherzer** kept the Astros offense quiet. Houston's late rally was not enough to prevent the upset.

GAME 2: Nationals 12, Astros 3

The shocks kept coming! Washington became the first team since 1999 to win the first two World Series games on the road. Their 17 total runs were the most in those games since 1960! **Kurt Suzuki's** homer gave the Astros a 3-2 lead and then they pounded the Nats bullpen, including a six-run seventh inning. **Adam Eaton** and **Michael A. Taylor** also hit homers for Washington.

GAME 3: Astros 4, Nationals 1

In the first World Series game played in

Washington D.C. since 1933, Houston sent Nats fans home unhappy. Astros pitching, led by starter **Zack Greinke**, shut down the Nationals powerful offense. Houston relievers allowed only two hits in four-plus innings of work. C **Robinson Chirinos**' homer helped power the 'Stros.

GAME 4: **Astros 8, Nationals 1**

Houston's surprise starter, **José Urquidy**, shut down the Nationals on two hits in five innings. 3B **Alex Bregman's** grand slam in the seventh sealed the game as Houston tied the Series, 2–2.

GAME 5: **Astros 7, Nationals 1**

Houston completed a sweep of D.C. thanks to three two-run homers–by **Yordan Álvarez**, **Carlos Correa**, and **George Springer**. Cole struck out nine and allowed only three hits to send the Astros back home one win away from the championship.

GAME 6: **Nationals 7, Astros 2**

Houston got two quick runs off Washington starter **Stephen Strasburg**. Then his pitching coach told him that he was "tipping" his pitches. That is, Strasburg was moving his hands in a way that showed what pitch was coming. Strasburg changed his motion and shut down the Astros! He pitched into the ninth inning and didn't allow another run. Meanwhile, 3B **Anthony Rendon** drove in five runs to send the Series to a Game 7!

GAME 7: **Nationals 6, Astros 2**

For the first time in major sports history, the road team won all seven games in a series! The Nationals captured their first World Series with another great comeback. The Astros left 10 men on base, leaving the door open for the Nats. Washington got a huge two-run homer from **Howie Kendrick** to take the lead 3–2. Then Houston's bullpen allowed three more runs and the Nats closed out a huge win. Strasburg was named the MVP for his big wins in Games 2 and 6.

Strasburg's big wins made him the MVP.

2019 Award Winners

Mike Trout

MOST VALUABLE PLAYER
AL: **Mike Trout**, ANGELS
NL: **Cody Bellinger**, DODGERS

CY YOUNG AWARD
AL: **Justin Verlander**, ASTROS
NL: **Jacob deGrom**, METS

ROOKIE OF THE YEAR
AL: **Yordan Álvarez**, ASTROS
NL: **Pete Alonso**, METS

MANAGER OF THE YEAR
AL: **Rocco Baldelli**, TWINS
NL: **Mike Shildt**, CARDINALS

HANK AARON AWARD (OFFENSE)
AL: **Mike Trout**, ANGELS
NL: **Christian Yelich**, BREWERS

ROBERTO CLEMENTE AWARD (COMMUNITY SERVICE)
Carlos Carrasco, INDIANS

Stat Champs

AL Hitting Leaders

48 HR
Jorge Soler, Royals

123 RBI
José Abreu, White Sox

.335 BATTING AVERAGE
Tim Anderson, White Sox

206 HITS
Whit Merrifield, Royals

46 STOLEN BASES
Mallex Smith, Mariners

NL Hitting Leaders

53 HOME RUNS
Pete Alonso, Mets

126 RBI
Anthony Rendon, Nationals

.329 BATTING AVERAGE
Christian Yelich, Brewers

189 HITS
Ozzie Albies, Braves

37 STOLEN BASES
Ronald Acuña Jr., Braves

AL Pitching Leaders

21 WINS
Justin Verlander, Astros

2.50 ERA
Gerrit Cole, Astros

38 SAVES
Roberto Osuna, Astros

326 STRIKEOUTS
Gerrit Cole, Astros

NL Pitching Leaders

18 WINS
Stephen Strasburg, Nationals

2.32 ERA
Hyun-Jin Ryu, Dodgers

255 STRIKEOUTS
Jacob deGrom, Mets

41 SAVES
Kirby Yates, Padres

Pete Alonso

MLB Crystal Baseball!

Looking ahead to 2021, who are some of the hottest young players to watch for? See if our crystal baseball was seeing clearly as we predict the top rookies of 2021! Some of them might have even had a chance in 2020.

WANDER FRANCO: The Tampa Bay SS might have ended up with the 2020 Rookie of the Year award. If he didn't, then he's the favorite for the honor in 2021. He's one of the top prospects in years, a great combo of offense and defense.

BOBBY WITT JR.: Another shortstop aiming for the top, Witt will be on the Royals' infield for years. He's got good genes; his dad was an 16-year MLB pitcher.

JULIO RODRIGUEZ: Yes, it's J-Rod! This Seattle outfielder has impressed fans wherever he plays. He'll be a Mariners favorite in 2021.

ADLEY RUTSCHMAN: Chosen No. 1 overall by the Baltimore Orioles in 2019, his road to the Majors was slowed without minor-league baseball in 2020. However, he has the slugging skills to perhaps crack the big-league lineup in 2021.

Julio Rodriguez

We had to print this book before baseball was supposed to start on July 24. Here's hoping they had a great season. If MLB played, enter the World Series winner here:

_____

Wander Franco

2020 Hall of Fame

The ceremony at Cooperstown, New York, was postponed to 2021. That doesn't mean we can't celebrate the newest members of baseball's most famous club.

DEREK JETER
Talk about hot starts! In 1996, Derek Jeter was the AL Rookie of the Year. He helped the Yankees win the World Series, too. New York made the playoffs in each of the next 11 years, led by the man they called "The Captain." Overall, Jeter won five championships with the Bronx Bombers. He was a top-notch leader, a clutch hitter, and became a standout defensive shortstop, too. His 3,465 career hits are sixth all-time. He played in 14 All-Star Games and won five Gold Gloves. No wonder he got into the Hall with 99.7 percent of the vote!

TED SIMMONS
You're doing something right if you play catcher in the Majors for 21 seasons. Simmons did just that, mostly for the Cardinals and Brewers. His bat kept him going, with a .285 career average that is among the best for catchers. He had eight seasons of .300 or better, with a high of .332 in 1975, and he made nine All-Star Games.

LARRY WALKER
For most of the second half of the 1990s, Walker was one of the game's most feared sluggers. He was a rare combination of power and batting skill, leading the NL in average three times. Once was in 1997, when he also led the league with 49 homers and was named MVP. He starred first for the old Montreal Expos. Moving to Colorado, he

Jeter will be inducted into the Hall in 2021.

took full advantage of that hitter's park. He also had one of the best outfield throwing arms around.

MARVIN MILLER
Miller never played a game, but he had a huge affect on the players. He led the players' union from 1966 to 1982. During that time, players gained the right to be free agents. He helped create the contracts that have led to today's enormous salaries for players.

World Series Winners

YEAR	WINNER	RUNNER-UP	SCORE*	YEAR	WINNER	RUNNER-UP	SCORE*
2019	Washington Nationals	Houston Astros	4–3	1991	Minnesota Twins	Atlanta Braves	4–3
2018	Boston Red Sox	Los Angeles Dodgers	4–1	1990	Cincinnati Reds	Oakland Athletics	4–0
2017	Houston Astros	Los Angeles Dodgers	4–3	1989	Oakland Athletics	San Francisco Giants	4–0
2016	Chicago Cubs	Cleveland Indians	4–3	1988	Los Angeles Dodgers	Oakland Athletics	4–1
2015	Kansas City Royals	New York Mets	4–1	1987	Minnesota Twins	St. Louis Cardinals	4–3
2014	San Francisco Giants	Kansas City Royals	4–3	1986	New York Mets	Boston Red Sox	4–3
2013	Boston Red Sox	St. Louis Cardinals	4–2	1985	Kansas City Royals	St. Louis Cardinals	4–3
2012	San Francisco Giants	Detroit Tigers	4–0	1984	Detroit Tigers	San Diego Padres	4–1
2011	St. Louis Cardinals	Texas Rangers	4–3	1983	Baltimore Orioles	Philadelphia Phillies	4–1
2010	San Francisco Giants	Texas Rangers	4–1	1982	St. Louis Cardinals	Milwaukee Brewers	4–3
2009	New York Yankees	Philadelphia Phillies	4–2	1981	Los Angeles Dodgers	New York Yankees	4–2
2008	Philadelphia Phillies	Tampa Bay Rays	4–1	1980	Philadelphia Phillies	Kansas City Royals	4–2
2007	Boston Red Sox	Colorado Rockies	4–0	1979	Pittsburgh Pirates	Baltimore Orioles	4–3
2006	St. Louis Cardinals	Detroit Tigers	4–1	1978	New York Yankees	Los Angeles Dodgers	4–2
2005	Chicago White Sox	Houston Astros	4–0	1977	New York Yankees	Los Angeles Dodgers	4–2
2004	Boston Red Sox	St. Louis Cardinals	4–0	1976	Cincinnati Reds	New York Yankees	4–0
2003	Florida Marlins	New York Yankees	4–2	1975	Cincinnati Reds	Boston Red Sox	4–3
2002	Anaheim Angels	San Francisco Giants	4–3	1974	Oakland Athletics	Los Angeles Dodgers	4–1
2001	Arizona Diamondbacks	New York Yankees	4–3	1973	Oakland Athletics	New York Mets	4–3
2000	New York Yankees	New York Mets	4–1	1972	Oakland Athletics	Cincinnati Reds	4–3
1999	New York Yankees	Atlanta Braves	4–0	1971	Pittsburgh Pirates	Baltimore Orioles	4–3
1998	New York Yankees	San Diego Padres	4–0	1970	Baltimore Orioles	Cincinnati Reds	4–1
1997	Florida Marlins	Cleveland Indians	4–3	1969	New York Mets	Baltimore Orioles	4–1
1996	New York Yankees	Atlanta Braves	4–2	1968	Detroit Tigers	St. Louis Cardinals	4–3
1995	Atlanta Braves	Cleveland Indians	4–2	1967	St. Louis Cardinals	Boston Red Sox	4–3
1993	Toronto Blue Jays	Philadelphia Phillies	4–2	1966	Baltimore Orioles	Los Angeles Dodgers	4–0
1992	Toronto Blue Jays	Atlanta Braves	4–2	1965	Los Angeles Dodgers	Minnesota Twins	4–3

* Score is represented in games played.

YEAR	WINNER	RUNNER-UP	SCORE*	YEAR	WINNER	RUNNER-UP	SCORE*
1964	St. Louis Cardinals	New York Yankees	4-3	1933	New York Giants	Washington Senators	4-1
1963	Los Angeles Dodgers	New York Yankees	4-0	1932	New York Yankees	Chicago Cubs	4-0
1962	New York Yankees	San Francisco Giants	4-3	1931	St. Louis Cardinals	Philadelphia Athletics	4-3
1961	New York Yankees	Cincinnati Reds	4-1	1930	Philadelphia Athletics	St. Louis Cardinals	4-2
1960	Pittsburgh Pirates	New York Yankees	4-3	1929	Philadelphia Athletics	Chicago Cubs	4-1
1959	Los Angeles Dodgers	Chicago White Sox	4-2	1928	New York Yankees	St. Louis Cardinals	4-0
1958	New York Yankees	Milwaukee Braves	4-3	1927	New York Yankees	Pittsburgh Pirates	4-0
1957	Milwaukee Braves	New York Yankees	4-3	1926	St. Louis Cardinals	New York Yankees	4-3
1956	New York Yankees	Brooklyn Dodgers	4-3	1925	Pittsburgh Pirates	Washington Senators	4-3
1955	Brooklyn Dodgers	New York Yankees	4-3	1924	Washington Senators	New York Giants	4-3
1954	New York Giants	Cleveland Indians	4-0	1923	New York Yankees	New York Giants	4-2
1953	New York Yankees	Brooklyn Dodgers	4-2	1922	New York Giants	New York Yankees	4-0
1952	New York Yankees	Brooklyn Dodgers	4-3	1921	New York Giants	New York Yankees	5-3
1951	New York Yankees	New York Giants	4-2	1920	Cleveland Indians	Brooklyn Robins	5-2
1950	New York Yankees	Philadelphia Phillies	4-0	1919	Cincinnati Reds	Chicago White Sox	5-3
1949	New York Yankees	Brooklyn Dodgers	4-1	1918	Boston Red Sox	Chicago Cubs	4-2
1948	Cleveland Indians	Boston Braves	4-2	1917	Chicago White Sox	New York Giants	4-2
1947	New York Yankees	Brooklyn Dodgers	4-3	1916	Boston Red Sox	Brooklyn Robins	4-1
1946	St. Louis Cardinals	Boston Red Sox	4-3	1915	Boston Red Sox	Philadelphia Phillies	4-1
1945	Detroit Tigers	Chicago Cubs	4-3	1914	Boston Braves	Philadelphia Athletics	4-0
1944	St. Louis Cardinals	St. Louis Browns	4-2	1913	Philadelphia Athletics	New York Giants	4-1
1943	New York Yankees	St. Louis Cardinals	4-1	1912	Boston Red Sox	New York Giants	4-3
1942	St. Louis Cardinals	New York Yankees	4-1	1911	Philadelphia Athletics	New York Giants	4-2
1941	New York Yankees	Brooklyn Dodgers	4-1	1910	Philadelphia Athletics	Chicago Cubs	4-1
1940	Cincinnati Reds	Detroit Tigers	4-3	1909	Pittsburgh Pirates	Detroit Tigers	4-3
1939	New York Yankees	Cincinnati Reds	4-0	1908	Chicago Cubs	Detroit Tigers	4-1
1938	New York Yankees	Chicago Cubs	4-0	1907	Chicago Cubs	Detroit Tigers	4-0
1937	New York Yankees	New York Giants	4-1	1906	Chicago White Sox	Chicago Cubs	4-2
1936	New York Yankees	New York Giants	4-2	1905	New York Giants	Philadelphia Athletics	4-1
1935	Detroit Tigers	Chicago Cubs	4-2	1903	Boston Americans	Pittsburgh Pirates	5-3
1934	St. Louis Cardinals	Detroit Tigers	4-3				

Note: 1904 not played because NL-champion Giants refused to play; 1994 not played due to MLB work stoppage.

COLLEGE BASKETBALL

BACK ON TOP!
South Carolina ended the 2019–20 college basketball season on top. They were also No. 1 in 2017. Unlike that first win, though, they didn't cut down the nets at the end of the season. Without an NCAA Tournament, the polls made the call. Tyasha Harris (with trophy) and the Gamecocks team got all but four first-place votes to earn the school's second national title.

A Year Without Madness

The 2019–20 college basketball season was already looking pretty wacky as the annual tournaments got closer. Then, all of a sudden, the tourneys were no more. College hoops ended a wild year in even wilder fashion. Fans and players alike were sad to go without March Madness.

Even after the games were stopped due to COVID-19, one thing was certain—hoops fans had been treated to a lot of exciting basketball. Everyone looked back on a men's season that saw more No. 1 teams than ever. They remembered a women's season that featured one of the best players of all time and saw a surprise "fall" by one of the top schools of all time.

On the men's side, the turnover at the top was amazing. In the first three months of the season, seven different teams reached No. 1—and each then lost a game! Baylor became the seventh No. 1 team, jumping over Gonzaga in late January. Not since the 1948–49 season had men's college hoops had that many different No. 1 teams.

The trend continued all season. It seemed like no one wanted to be on top! On February 22, Nos. 1, 2, and 4 all lost. No. 1 Baylor fell and No. 2 Gonzaga was shocked by BYU. Undefeated No. 4 San Diego State lost its first game of the year, 66–63 to UNLV. Meanwhile, surprise team Dayton ended the season at No. 3, the school's highest ranking ever.

Baylor (right) shocked Connecticut with a historic loss.

Kansas rose above the rest!

When the regular season ended, Kansas wound up on top. The Jayhawks ended the season with a 16-game winning streak. The school's biggest victory came with a win over then-No. 1 Baylor in late February.

The big news in women's college basketball was the "fall" of Connecticut. For the first time since 2007, the Huskies were NOT in the final top four. They ended up ranked No. 5. After a surprise loss to Baylor (page 79), UConn lost to **Sabrina Ionescu** and Oregon in February. South Carolina handed the Huskies a third loss.

Into the space left by UConn stepped a solid South Carolina team and an exciting Oregon squad. Freshman of the year, and second-team All-America, **Aliyah Boston**, was the star for SC. Ionescu (see page 80) and **Ruthy Hebard** were both first-team All-Americas for Oregon.

And in a season that ended too soon, let's give a shout-out to Hartford's women's team. The school had lost 28 games in a row and was playing the conference champion, Stony Brook, in the final game of the regular season. But Hartford gave underdogs everywhere a boost by winning its first game! It turned out to be the perfect way to wrap up a strange season!

FINAL MEN'S TOP 10
Associated Press

1. Kansas
2. Gonzaga
3. Dayton
4. Florida State
5. Baylor
6. San Diego State
7. Creighton
8. Kentucky
9. Michigan State
10. Villanova

FINAL WOMEN'S TOP 10
Associated Press

1. South Carolina
2. Oregon
3. Baylor
4. Maryland
5. Connecticut
6. Louisville
7. Stanford
8. North Carolina State
9. Mississippi State
10. UCLA

Arizona State (in white) pulled off a double upset, beating both Oregon schools in a weekend!

Hoops Notes

EARLY UPSETS:
The upsets started early in a surprising 2019–20 season. In only its third game, No. 1 Kentucky was shocked by Evansville at home. The Wildcats were 25-point favorites and had never lost when ranked No. 1 and hosting a non-conference opponent (they were 39–0!). Three weeks later, Duke had taken over the No. 1 spot–but was shocked by Stephen F. Austin. The winners were 27.5-point underdogs, making their win the biggest upset in 15 years.

When ranked No. 1, Duke had *never* lost to a team outside of the top conferences before.

COMEBACK CITY:
TCU trailed No. 2 Baylor late in the game, but an 18–1 scoring burst turned things around. The Horned Frogs celebrated on their home court after nailing down the 75–72 win. **Desmond Bane** was the big scorer for TCU; he scored 23 points, including 17 in the final 12 minutes of the game.

LAST SHOT:
USC guard **Jonah Mathews** had high hopes for his senior season. He never thought that his final shot for the Trojans would turn out to be such a memorable one. With one second left, he buried a three-point shot that gave his team a 54–52 win over archrival UCLA. USC had also beaten UCLA the first time these teams played in January. It was the first time the Trojans had swept the Bruins since 2016.

DUCKS TOP YANKS:
Team USA is made up of the top women's players in the nation. Stars from the WNBA and international leagues play tournaments like the Olympics. They need practice, of course, so they sometimes take on college teams. USA usually wins, but not in 2020. **Sabrina Ionescu** led Oregon to a shocking 93–86 win. It was only the second time ever that a college team beat the national team.

STREAK SNAPPED:
Connecticut was invincible on its home court. The women's team had won 98 straight there, dating back to 2013. On January 9, Baylor snapped that streak, crushing the Huskies 74–58. It was also UConn's first loss of the season and came one game short of tying their own 99-game record!

SOUTHERN SURPRISE:
Winning at the right time really helps. In mid-January, Baylor's women's team beat No. 1 UConn. The same week, No. 2 Oregon fell to Arizona State. ASU then knocked off No. 3 Oregon State for an incredible double upset! When the dust cleared, South Carolina had jumped from No. 4 to the top spot. They didn't lose the rest of the way and claimed the unofficial national title. Good timing!

USC's Mathews made magic!

Players of the Year!

Sabrina Ionescu
Guard • Oregon

AWARDS

Wooden Award*
Naismith Player of the Year
AP Player of the Year
Wade Trophy
All-America First Team

▶ **First NCAA player ever, man or woman, with 2,000 points, 1,000 rebounds, and 1,000 assists in a college career.**

▶ **All-time NCAA leader in triple-double games, men or women, with 26**

▶ **2019–20 led NCAA in assists (9.1 per game)**

▶ **All-time leading scorer in Oregon history**

*Also won in 2019, sixth woman ever to go back-to-back

Obi Toppin
Forward • Dayton

AWARDS

**Wooden Award
Naismith Award
AP Player of the Year
NABC Player of the Year
Karl Malone Award***

▶ **Full name: Obadiah**

▶ **Averaged 20.0 points and 7.5 rebounds per game**

▶ **Shot better than 63 percent**

▶ **Led Dayton to highest ranking ever**

▶ **Seventh sophomore to win Wooden Award**

*Top power forward

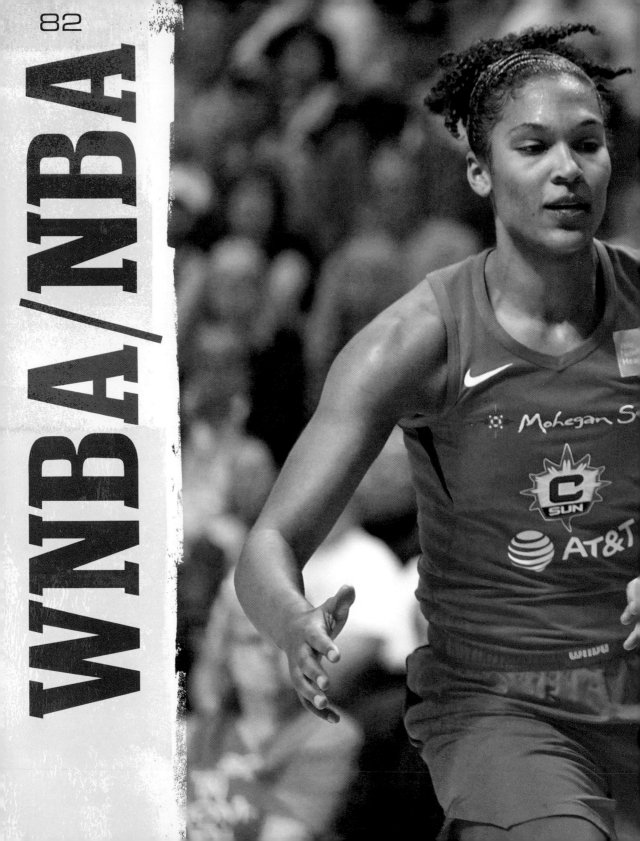

WNBA/NBA

WINNERS IN WASHINGTON!
Washington capped off a tremendous 2019 WNBA season with a thrilling Game 5 win over Connecticut. Superstar Elena Delle Donne finally captured her first pro title. Read more about a great WNBA season (and part of a super NBA season) inside!

2019 WNBA

The biggest WNBA story in 2019 was that more and more people were enjoying the story! TV ratings and social media presence were way up. WNBA players were part of the 2K20 basketball video game for the first time. And lots more NBA players were declaring themselves fans of the oldest women's pro sports league in the country!

Unfortunately, injuries were a big story in the WNBA in 2019, too. Defending MVP **Breanna Stewart** was out for the season with a knee injury. All-star superstar **Diana Taurasi** missed 28 games. **Sue Bird**, another all-timer, missed the season for Seattle as well. Meanwhile, in Minnesota, **Maya Moore** took a year off from playing to focus on her ministry work.

Napheesa Collier put together an award-winning rookie season for the Lynx.

Sky superstars faced off as All-Stars.

2019 WNBA Standings

EASTERN CONFERENCE

Washington Mystics	26–8
Connecticut Sun	23–11
Chicago Sky	20–14
Indiana Fever	13–21
New York Liberty	10–24
Atlanta Dream	8–26

WESTERN CONFERENCE

Los Angeles Sparks	22–12
Las Vegas Aces	21–13
Seattle Storm	18–16
Minnesota Lynx	18–16
Phoenix Mercury	15–19
Dallas Wings	10–24

Other stars rose to take their places, however. Washington's **Elena Delle Donne** won her second WNBA MVP award and led the Mystics to their best regular-season record ever. WNBA Rookie of the Year **Napheesa Collier** stepped in for the Lynx to replace Moore as a top scorer. The Chicago Sky had one of its best seasons led by guards **Courtney Vandersloot** and **Allie Quigley**. Out West, the Las Vegas Aces continued their hot play, led by young star **A'ja Wilson** and veteran center **Liz Cambage**.

The playoffs got good ratings and featured some awesome basketball . . . and great TV ratings! See page 87 to find out which team won its first-ever WNBA title!

WNBA AWARDS WINNERS

MVP: **Elena Delle Donne**, Washington
ROOKIE OF THE YEAR: **Napheesa Collier**, Minnesota
DEFENSIVE PLAYER OF THE YEAR: **Natasha Howard**, Seattle
SIXTH WOMAN: **Dearica Hamby**, Las Vegas
MOST IMPROVED PLAYER: **Leilani Mitchell**, Phoenix
KIM PERROT SPORTSMANSHIP AWARD: **Nneka Ogwumike**, L.A.

Jasmine Thomas (left) and Connecticut surprised the mighty LA Sparks.

WNBA Playoffs

First Round

Chicago and Seattle won the first-round single-elimination games. Seattle's **Jordin Canada** scored 26 in the Storm's win over the Lynx. Chicago knocked out the Mercury, helped in part by an injury to Phoenix star, **Brittney Griner**.

Second Round

Las Vegas won a thriller over the Sky when **Dearica Hamby** hit a game-winning 35-foot three-pointer in the final seconds to win by a point! Seattle's season ended when the Los Angeles Sparks used a powerful offense to win by 23 points. **Chelsea Gray** led the way with 23 points.

Conference Semifinals

Connecticut 3, Los Angeles 0

The Sun swept through the powerful Sparks lineup. In the third game, the Sparks played All-Star **Candace Parker** for only 11 minutes, a choice that had fans wondering why. In that game, Connecticut's **Jasmine Thomas** had a career-high 29 points.

Washington 3, Las Vegas 1

The Mystics' terrific trio **Elena Delle Donne** (25), **Emma Meesseman** (22), and **Kristi Toliver** (20) set a record as the first teammates to each go for at least 20 in a playoff-best-of-5 clincher. The series win sent Washington back to the WNBA Finals.

2019 WNBA Finals

GAME 1 Washington 95, Connecticut 86

Having the WNBA MVP on your team is a good way to win! **Elena Delle Donne**, fresh off picking up her trophy, scored 22 points as her team won its first-ever WNBA Finals game. **Ariel Atkins** added 21 for a one-two scoring punch.

GAME 2 Connecticut 99 Washington 87

Jonquel Jones showed that she has MVP stuff, too. The Sun forward became the first player ever with 30 points and 15 rebounds in a WNBA Finals game. **Delle Donne** went out in the first half with a back problem and the Sun took advantage.

GAME 3 Washington 94 Connecticut 81

Delle Donne played through pain to lead her team to a big Game 3 win. **Emma Meesseman** (21) and **Kristi Toliver** (20) picked up the scoring, while Donne contributed 13 points . . . and a lot of inspiration.

GAME 4 Connecticut 90 Washington 86

You can't win if you can't score. The Sun did not allow a single Mystics point for more than the final two minutes and held on for the series-tying win. Connecticut's **Alyssa Thomas** nearly had the first-ever WNBA Finals triple-double with 17 points, 11 assists, and 8 rebounds.

GAME 5 Washington 89 Connecticut 78

Washington won its first WNBA championship thanks to the one-two power of **Meesseman** (22 points) and **Delle Donne** (21). "It feels phenomenal, my goodness, it feels so good," said Donne about earning her first ring. Washington trailed by nine in the second half before mounting a big comeback. Meesseman was named the WNBA Finals MVP after averaging 17.8 points and 4.6 rebounds per game.

Delle Donne scores for the Mystics.

NBA: The Short Season

By the time you read this, we hope the NBA is back in action or has wrapped up a great 2019–20 season. But we had to finish this book before we knew all the answers.

One thing was for sure: Fans were jazzed (and we don't just mean in Utah!) about the season. Before it started, a large group of top stars changed jerseys and remade the NBA in a small group of two-star teams.

Anthony Davis joined **LeBron James** with the Lakers to create the first mega-team. **Kawhi Leonard** left Toronto and hopped onto the Clippers to pair with **Paul George**. **Kevin Durant** left the Warriors to head East for the Nets along with star guard **Kyrie Irving**. **Russell Westbrook** was traded from Oklahoma City to Houston, where he could feed the ball to super-scorer **James Harden**.

Before the season was cut short, there were some great highlights to remember. The

Anthony Davis (left) and LeBron James formed a powerful duo in Los Angeles.

NBA HORSE

While fans watched from home, NBA stars tried to keep entertaining. A group of pros, including some WNBA heroes, staged an epic HORSE tournament using their phones and video meeting apps. Sixteen current or former players went head-to-head in the classic playground game of "can you top this?" In the end, the winner was **Mike Conley** of the Utah Jazz, who knocked off **Zach LaVine** when the Chicago Bulls star couldn't match the final shot, a layup from behind the backboard.

Milwaukee Bucks fell short of reaching the 2019 NBA Finals, but looked like they were aiming to try again. When play stopped, they had the best record in the NBA and **Giannis Antetokounmpo** was again playing to MVP form. Milwaukee reeled off an 18-game winning streak in November and December. A big surprise in the East was the Miami Heat. **Jimmy Butler** was leading them to a great season, a big jump from 2018–19 when they didn't even make the playoffs. Toronto, the defending champ, showed there was life after Leonard. They trailed only the Bucks in the East thanks to **Kyle Lowry** and **Pascal Siakam**.

In the West, the Lakers were on top. The addition of Davis gave LeBron the support he needed. Incredibly, he was still scoring a high pace but was also leading the NBA in assists! The Lakers got off to the hottest start in team history, 24–3. Meanwhile, the Clippers were just behind them at 21–8. Things were heating up as the playoffs neared. How did it all end up? You know better than we do!

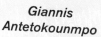

Giannis Antetokounmpo

More NBA Notes

Here Comes Zion:
No. 1 draft pick **Zion Williamson** of the New Orleans Pelicans didn't start play until January 22 due to a knee injury. He was worth the wait. In his first game, he scored 17 of his 22 points in the fourth quarter. In 19 games, he averaged 23.6 points and 6.8 rebounds. He reached double figures in scoring in every game. But mostly, he thrilled fans with a series of spectacular dunks.

50 Points, No W:
Kyrie Irving had a memorable first game with the Nets, scoring a Brooklyn-record 50 points. But it was not enough for the win, as Minnesota came back to beat the Nets 127–126 in OT.

◀ Pile on the Points:
In a November game, the Houston Rockets and Washington Wizards lit up the scoreboard. Houston's **James Harden** led the way with 59 points. It was a good thing he didn't stop at 57. Houston won by only one point, 159–158. It was the most points ever in an NBA game decided by a single point. Washington also set a tough record. They matched the most points ever for a losing team in a non-overtime game.

NBA 2K
You play basketball video games. The stars play basketball video games! Another virus-timeout activity was a fun online video contest among NBA stars. The flying fingers of **Devin Booker** and **Deandre Ayton** made the final, with Booker earning the virtual victory!

Kobe Bryant, 1978-2020

The whole sports world was saddened on January 26, 2020. Retired NBA superstar Kobe Bryant, his daughter Gianna, and seven other people were killed in a helicopter crash in California. They were on their way to one of Gianna's basketball games. Bryant was an 18-time All-Star and No. 4 all-time in scoring in league history. He had led the Los Angeles Lakers to five NBA titles, thrilling fans with his intensity, drive, and will to win. In retirement, he continued his winning ways, writing children's books, making movies, and helping young athletes.

In his short life, the player known as "Mamba" had touched millions of fans around the world. The shocking end to Bryant's life hit a lot of people hard. Fans poured onto the streets around the Staples Center, home of Kobe's Los Angeles Lakers team. The internet lit up as tributes poured in from every corner of the world. Barack Obama, Tiger Woods, Mike Trout, and Magic Johnson were among the thousands who shared memories. The entertainment world was touched, too, as music and movie stars shared their sadness.

The NBA honored Kobe at the All-Star Game in February. One team wore No. 2, Gianna's number. The other team wore No. 24, one of Kobe's two jersey numbers. On February 24 (2/24, using the numbers again), Staples Center in Los Angeles was packed for a touching memorial. Speaker after speaker praised Kobe for his skills, his heart, and his generosity.

In April, Kobe Bryant was elected to the Basketball Hall of Fame.

He will be terribly missed, but his inspiration will remain for years to come.

Kobe's Greatness

* All-Star Game MVP
  2002, 2007, 2009, 2011
* NBA MVP 2008
* NBA Finals MVP 2009, 2010
* 18 All-Star Games
* 10-time First-Team All-NBA

SOCCER

SUPER SCORER

Mexican star Carlos Vela continued to take MLS by storm. In his and LAFC's second season ever, he set a scoring record and led the team to one of the best seasons in league history. They didn't win it all, though, so look for them to come back for more!

2019 MLS

The big story in MLS 2019 was LAFC, which set an all-time record for most points (72) and tied a record for most goals (85). Forward **Carlos Vela** also set a single-season record with 34 goals. But fans in the future will look back on 2019 as the season that Seattle ended up the champion. What happened? A shocking semifinal playoff loss ruined LAFC's dream season.

Another big story was on LA's other team, the Galaxy. The international superstar **Zlatan Ibrahimović** continued his powerhouse run in MLS. He became only the third player in league history to reach 30 goals, trailing only Vela in 2019. "Ibra" filled the press with great quotes, and filled the goal with amazing shots, such as his "karate kick" goal against Toronto. It was the 500th of his long career.

Whenever the 2020 MLS season re-started, the league welcomed new teams in Miami and Nashville. In 2021, teams will start play in Charlotte, and Austin, Texas.

El Trafíco Lives Up to Hype

This huge game was between two teams from Los Angeles. Galaxy is a five-time champ. LAFC is just two years old and had never beaten the Galaxy. In front of a packed house, the two teams played an exciting, high-scoring game. LAFC's **Carlos Vela** scored twice and **Adama Diomande** came on with two goals in the second half. Galaxy star **Zlatan Ibrahimović** scored a goal, too, but it was not enough and LAFC held for an exciting win.

CONFERENCE FINALS
Seattle 3, LAFC 1
Seattle shocked LAFC in front of a stunned Los Angeles crowd. The Sounders shut down LAFC's record-setting offense. **Raúl Ruidíaz** scored twice for the Sounders, and they earned their second MLS Cup berth in three seasons. LAFC, meanwhile, wandered off the field, not sure what had happened to their dream season.

MLS CUP
Seattle 3, Toronto 1
These two teams met for the title for the third time in four seasons. Their mini-series was tied at one game apiece, and Seattle broke the tie to win its second MLS championship. Toronto dominated the game for more than 60 minutes, outshooting and outplaying the home team. A deflected goal for Seattle broke the 0–0 tie, however. The Sounders added two more and their fans were able to celebrate with the team.

2019 NWSL

Nearly every NWSL team welcomed back members of the World Cup–winning US team. Those players played key roles in helping four teams reach the semifinals. But the United States was not the only team with international stars in the NWSL. Players from 11 countries took part in America's longest-lasting women's pro soccer league.

SEMIFINAL 1
Courage 4, Reign 1

Seattle, led by **Megan Rapinoe**, almost pulled off a huge upset over the defending champs. There was no score until the 87th minute when the Courage earned a penalty kick that **Heather O'Reilly** buried. Seattle then shocked the Courage crowd with a goal in stoppage time by **Ifeoma Onumonu**. In extra time, though, North Carolina roared. **Debinha** scored a great free-kick goal and then the Reign let in an own goal. The Courage's **Crystal Dunn** then sealed the win with a left-footed shot.

SEMIFINAL 2
Red Stars 1, Thorns 0

The Red Stars had been to four previous NWSL semifinals. They had lost every one of them. This time, however, thanks to US stars **Julie Ertz** and **Tierna Davidson**, Chicago brought home the win. They got the only goal they needed in the eighth minute from Australian superstar **Sam Kerr**, and then held on for the big win.

CHAMPIONSHIP GAME
Courage 4, Red Stars 0

North Carolina was just too much for the Red Stars. Brazilian star Debhina scored in the fourth minute and a rout was on. The Courage won their second NWSL championship in a row in front of their home fans. US Women's National Team members **Jessica McDonald**, **Sam Mewis**, and Dunn also scored for North Carolina. The four goals were the most ever in a NWSL championship game.

A new dynasty? Carolina made it back-to-back titles in NWSL with a rout of the Red Stars.

2019 Players of the Year

MEGAN RAPINOE
United States/Seattle Reign

"Pino" led the US women's team to another World Cup championship in the summer of 2019. She won the tournament MVP award as well as the Golden Boot as top scorer. Rapinoe also became a leading voice in the women's team's ongoing fight for equal pay. In December, she was also just the fourth woman ever to be named *Sports Illustrated's* Sportsperson of the Year.

LIONEL MESSI
Argentina/FC Barcelona

The amazing Argentine goal-scorer added another to his very long list of trophies. Messi won his sixth Ballon d'Or, a new record and one more than rival **Cristiano Ronaldo**. Messi led Barcelona to the Spanish League title, was the top scorer in Spain and in Europe for the season, and scored 12 goals in Champions League play.

KYLE IS KING

Kyle Busch had not won a NASCAR race in 21 starts. He broke that streak at just the right time. After earning his way into the Chase for the Cup final four, he won the Miami race to capture the Cup! He had to battle former Cup champs to win. Follow all the action inside!

NASCAR

Martin Truex Jr. came close, but couldn't land on top again.

NASCAR 2019

A tight pack of former NASCAR champions found themselves battling for the top spot for most of the season in 2019. **Kyle Busch** (2015 champ) won three of the first eight races, including an always-exciting battle in Bristol. Heading into the Chase for the Cup playoffs, Busch also led the way with five top-five finishes putting him atop the standings. He was followed by **Joey Logano** (2018 champ), and **Kevin Harvick** (2014 champ).

With wins at Charlotte and Sonoma, **Martin Truex, Jr.** (2017 champ) also reached four wins for the season. He roared into the top five in points as the playoff chase began. **Brad Keselowski** (2012 champ) lingered just outside the top five. He did win the second-most races in the regular season with three (Atlanta, Martinsville, Kansas).

Sneaking into this mix was a racer hoping to win his first NASCAR title. Veteran **Denny Hamlin** became the third driver with four race wins when he captured Pocono and second Bristol wins.

Meanwhile, **Justin Haley** and **Alex Bowman** (page 133) each captured their first NASCAR race wins. And speaking of firsts, **William Byron** made his first Chase for the Cup appearance. In perhaps one of the biggest surprises of the year, however, seven-time champ **Jimmie Johnson** was not part of the final group of 16 drivers. It was the first Chase for the Cup ever held without Johnson; the Chase started in 2004.

NASCAR, as usual, offered some excitement off the track. After a race in May, **Ryan Newman** and **Clint Bowyer** got into a fight beside pit road

CHASE FOR THE CUP!
2019 FINAL STANDINGS

PLACE/DRIVER (CAR NO.)

1. **Kyle BUSCH** (18)
2. **Martin TRUEX JR.** (19)
3. **Kevin HARVICK** (4)
4. **Denny HAMLIN** (11)
5. **Joey LOGANO** (22)
6. **Kyle LARSON** (42)
7. **Ryan BLANEY** (12)
8. **Brad KESELOWSKI** (2)
9. **Clint BOWYER** (14)
10. **Chase ELLIOTT** (9)
11. **William BYRON** (24)
12. **Alex BOWMAN** (88)

after they had bumped cars during the race!

Daniel Suarez and Michael McDonald had had an earlier scuffle after a race at Phoenix. Were NASCAR drivers trying to get a page in the boxing section of the Year in Sports?

In happier news, at Darlington in September, longtime NASCAR fans were thrilled by the Throwback paint schemes used by most teams. Recently retired superstar Dale Earnhardt Jr. made a surprise appearance at that race, too.

The final ten races included some surprise wins, a few close finishes, and set up a championship race that included three former champs . . . just as expected! In the end, just one of those drivers would add to his total of NASCAR season titles?

Read on to find out!

Young William Byron had a breakout season in 2019 and looks for more ahead!

2019 CHASE FOR THE CUP!

OPENING ROUND

LAS VEGAS: Martin Truex Jr. earned the first spot in the second round with a big win here. It gave him five for the season, the most by any driver to this point. Kevin Harvick was second, putting him in a good spot to advance, too.

RICHMOND: Make it two in a row for Truex. It was his sixth win of the season and second in 2019 at the track in Virginia. His Joe Gibbs Racing Team teammate Kyle Busch actually led the most laps, but finished second to Truex.

CHARLOTTE: On the challenging Roval course, Chase Elliott hit a barrier during a restart while leading the race on Lap 64! But he recovered to win and earn a spot in the next round. Ryan Newman saw his season end when he missed a turn and finished behind Alex Bowman.

Eliminated: Aric Almirola, Kurt Busch, Erik Jones, Ryan Newman.

Kyle Busch posed with his wife, Samantha, after flying his championship flag.

CHALLENGER ROUND

DOVER: Kyle Larson picked the right time to break a 75-race winless streak. His victory here put him into the next round. Larson had finished second nine times during the streak but had not gained a checkered flag since 2017.

TALLADEGA: Ryan Blaney made it to the Round of 8 by inches! He battled Ryan Newman down the stretch as cars collided behind them. Blaney was ahead by about a foot and only .007 seconds as they roared across the finish line.

KANSAS: A late restart helped Denny Hamlin win to lock up his spot in the next round. The final-lap crowd forced out former champ Brad Keselowski, however. The Round of 8 was set, and the race for the top spot remained wide open!

Eliminated: Alex Bowman, Clint Bowyer, William Byron, Brad Keselowski.

ROUND OF EIGHT

MARTINSVILLE: For the third straight season, Truex will have a shot at the championship. He earned his spot in the final with a solid victory at the famous short track in West Virginia. He got ahead early and led for 464 of the 500 laps.

TEXAS: Harvick must love the taste of Texas. He won here for the third year in a row. The victory sent him into the championship round. Harvick started from the pole but had to hold off Aric Almirola on the last lap to clinch the victory.

Elliott won at the Charlotte Roval.

PHOENIX: Hamlin is in! The veteran racer won at the Arizona track to clinch his spot in the final four. Former champ Kyle Busch earned the fourth spot for points he earned during the Chase for the Cup, even though he did not win any of the final 10 races.

NASCAR CHAMPIONSHIP

MIAMI: Kyle Busch broke a 21-race winless streak at the perfect time. He earned his second career season title by getting the checkered flag in the year's final race. His challengers were let down by mistakes on pit road. Truex was forced to go back after his team put tires on the incorrect wheels. And a piece of tape helped shut down the engine of Hamlin. Along with Busch, the other big winner was his Joe Gibbs Racing team. Gibbs had three of the final four (only Harvick was not on that team). Along with three of the top four, Gibbs earned its fifth championship all-time.

Other NASCAR Champs

About time! Crafton won his first title in five years.

Gander Outdoors Truck Series

Five years after winning his second truck title, **Matt Crafton** earned his third. He did it the hard way—the veteran didn't win a single race in 2019. He earned enough points to finish on top, including a second-place finish at the final race in Miami. Crafton now trails all-time leader **Roy Hornaday, Jr.**, who had four truck championships. At 43 years old, Crafton was older than all of the other final four contenders. He made sure to stay ahead of **Ross Chastain**, his closest competitor for the title on the final laps. Crafton played it smart late in the race once he knew how close Chastain was. "I had to race as hard as I could without doing anything dumb to put the thing in the fence," he laughed after the race.

XFINITY SERIES

For the second year in a row, **Tyler Reddick** brought home the checkered flag for the Xfinity season championship. Reddick led the last 19 laps of the Miami race. "It's all about this race team, man," Reddick said. "I'm losing my breath, I'm that excited. This one means so much more. It was really cool to go back-to-back."

Once again, **Cole Custer** trailed Reddick to the finish line and in series points. **Christopher Bell** led the year with eight wins, but was fifth in the final race after a mistake on pit road. Reddick won't make it three in a row. He'll drive in the Cup Series in 2020.

Bowman earned his first career win in a dominating Chicago race.

NASCAR Notes

Happy in the Rain

Justin Haley won his first NASCAR race—in only his third start—thanks to a big rainstorm. The July 2019 race at Daytona was shortened to only 127 laps after lightning struck the track with Haley in the lead. After waiting two hours, NASCAR canceled the rest of the race and Haley was a wet and happy winner.

First-Time Winner

Alex Bowman had come close to winning several times in his short NASCAR career. He even earned three second-place finishes in a row earlier in 2019. He finally drove under the checkered flag in July in Chicago for his first NASCAR victory. "I was just tired of running second," he said afterward.

A Close Call

In August 2019, NASCAR fans got a scare when popular former driver **Dale Earnhardt Jr.** and his family escaped without injury from a small-plane crash. Later that month, the retired superstar thrilled his fans by driving one more race, an Xfinity event at Darlington, one of his favorite tracks.

NASCAR 2020

Denny Hamlin won the 2020 Daytona 500 about a month before NASCAR paused for COVID-19. NASCAR roared back to the track on May 17 at Darlington. Other tracks were added to the schedule in June and July—all races were held without fans. NASCAR's biggest headlines came when the entire driver community rallied to support African American driver **Bubba Wallace** during the Black Lives Matter protests.

OTHER MOTOR SPORTS

DIRT CHURNIN'!

Motocross racers battle each other, but they also have to deal with a lot of mud! In 2019, Eli Tomac showed he was the best "mudder" around, winning his third AMA Motocross championship. Read on to find out about other racing champions—in and out of the mud!

Formula 1 2019

The Mercedes Formula 1 team got off to a rocket start in 2019. Defending champion **Lewis Hamilton** won six of the first eight races. His teammate **Valtteri Bottas** won the other two. Only when Red Bull's **Max Verstappen** won in Austria was the Mercedes streak beaten. In fact, if you add in races from 2018, Mercedes won 10 straight, the second-longest streak ever for a team. Verstappen added a second win at the German Grand Prix. The win in Germany was embarrassing for the Mercedes team in its home country. Hamilton spun out on the rainy track and crashed.

In between Verstappen's wins, **Hamilton** won the British Grand Prix in his home country. It was his sixth win at the historic raceway, the most ever by any driver.

In the race in Belgium, **Charles Leclerc** won his first F1 race (and Ferrari's first of the season). He dedicated the win to Formula 2 driver **Anthoine Hubert**,

Lewis Hamilton thrilled British racing fans with his second F1 drivers' title in a row.

Sebastian Vettlel tried to regain his championship form, but fell short in 2019.

who had been killed the previous week in a crash. Leclerc made it two in a row with a win in Italy. The victory was sweeter than usual for team owner Ferrari, which is based near the race track in Monza.

At the next race, in Singapore, a familiar face stood atop the podium. Germany's **Sebastian Vettel** has won four Formula 1 world titles, but hadn't even won a race in more than a year. In Singapore, though, he held on for the checkered flag and stayed in the hunt for title number five.

Hamilton roared back to the top in the race in Russia. His Mercedes teammate Bottas was second.

Mercedes earned another win at the race in Japan, but this time it was Bottas on top. The German carmaker clinched the trophy for top team, while Hamilton finished in third and padded his lead for the season driver's title. Two weeks later in Mexico, Hamilton was back where he belonged, leading the race at the end. Vettel was second followed by Bottas. Hamilton moved

farther ahead of the pack in the season standings with just three races left.

At the United States Grand Prix in Texas, Hamilton sealed the deal. With a second-place finish behind Bottas, the British star earned his sixth Formula 1 drivers' championship. That's the second-most ever behind Germany's **Michael Schumacher**, who had seven.

2019 FORMULA 1 TOP DRIVERS

PLACE/DRIVER/TEAM	POINTS
1. Lewis **HAMILTON**, Mercedes	413
2. Vallteri **BOTTAS**, Mercedes	326
3. Max **VERSTAPPEN**, Red Bull	278
4. Charles **LECLERC**, Ferrari	264
5. Sebastian **VETTEL**, Ferrari	240

Former champ Josef Newgarden was back on top in 2019.

IndyCar 2019

In racing, it's not how you start, it's how you finish. In the 2019 IndyCar season, **Alexander Rossi** roared out in the early going. He won at Long Beach after starting from the pole. Rossi won by an incredible 20 seconds. Soon after, he earned six straight top-five finishes including a second victory at Elkhart Lake. So he cruised to the season title, right?

Not so fast (pardon the pun!). Rossi gained only a pair of top-threes the rest of the way as well as several finishes far back and finished third overall. Meanwhile, **Josef Newgarden** was like the tortoise in the old story—slow and steady. He won the first race

of the season, but then watched Rossi fly by in the standings. At Fort Worth, however, Newgarden got back on top of the podium. He padded his lead with six top-five finishes in the second half of the season, including a win at Iowa. He moved into the top spot and never really looked back. The American won his second IndyCar title in three seasons. He got the clinching points in the final race at Laguna Seca.

Newgarden and Rossi were not the only drivers on the track, of course. Defending champ **Scott Dixon** won two races but had several wrecks that pushed him out of the title chase. **Simon Pagenaud** also won a trio of races, including the famous Indy 500, but didn't find enough points in other races to overtake Newgarden. Veteran **Will Power** won two of the final four races, but they were not enough, either.

Perhaps the biggest driver news was the success of young stars behind the wheel. In the season's second race, **Colton Herta** became the youngest IndyCar winner ever. He was just 18 when he won in Texas. He wrapped up a dream rookie season by winning the final race at Laguna Seca. Colton learned from the best. His father, **Bryan**, was a 13-year driver. Herta was good, but **Felix Rosenqvist** was the rookie of the year, finishing just ahead of Herta in total points.

INDYCAR 2019 FINAL STANDINGS

PLACE/DRIVER/COUNTRY	POINTS
1. **Josef Newgarden**, US	641
2. **Simon Pagenaud**, France	616
3. **Alexander Rossi**, US	608
4. **Scott Dixon**, New Zealand	578
5. **Will Power**, New Zealand	550
6. **Felix Rosenqvist**, Sweden	425
7. **Colton Herta**, US	420
Ryan Hunter-Reay, US	420
9. **Takuma Sato**, Japan	415
10. **Graham Rahal**, US	389

INDY 2020

The red flag dropped on IndyCar before it even got started in 2020. Racing roared back in June when **Scott Dixon** won at Texas (left). No fans were in the stands, of course, for everyone's safety. IndyCar planned 13 more races through late October. The famous Indy 500 was moved to August 23. It was hoped that fans would be welcome at that race, but details were still being worked out at press time. We hope you watched the big race, though! Write down who took home the checkered flag!

Drag Racing

FUNNY CAR

Robert Hight was the top of the heights in Funny Car for the second time in three seasons. He nipped **Matt Hagan** in the NHRA Finals semifinal race. That gave Hight enough points to win the season title. "That was the most important run of my life. When it comes down to one run to win a championship, how will you perform?" he asked afterward. He already knew the answer!

TOP FUEL

In Top Fuel, **Steve Torrence** took a similar path. A quarterfinal win earned him his second straight championship. The winning margin over **Brittany Force** was only .03 seconds! One more clean run in the next race and he was holding up the big trophy. A midseason five-event winning streak put Torrence in the spot to win.

PRO STOCK

The Pro Stock champ was another repeat winner. However, **Erica Enders** had not reached the top spot since 2015. A strong and steady 2019 season gave her a big lead entering the final event. A semifinal win by a tiny .004 seconds made her a three-time champ. She became the third woman ever with a trio of titles.

PRO STOCK MOTORCYCLE

Andrew Hines made a big mistake in his first race at the NHRA Finals and he was out after one round. The season points leader then watched as his rivals all failed to take advantage. Hines's short day on the track ended with his record-tying sixth season championship.

Erica Enders raced to the top in 2019.

Motorcycle Racing

Marc Marquez

MOTOCROSS

Eli Tomac started on top and stayed that way. In the 2019 AMA Motocross series, Tomac finished in the top three of every event but one. He piled up enough points to win his third season championship in a row in the 450 class. He capped the season off with a final-race victory at the annual Ironman National. In the 250 class, **Adam Cianciarulo** won seven events and made the final three at every outing. At the Ironman final, he stayed just ahead of rival **Dylan Ferrandis** to win his first national championship.

2019 MOTO GP

Marc Márquez might be the most famous international athlete you've never heard of. His sport, Moto GP—high-speed track motorcycle racing—is not big in the United States. But in the internationally popular sport, with races in 18 countries, Marquez is the LeBron James or the Tom Brady. Though he is only 26, Marquez has captured eight world championships, including six at the sport's highest level. He clinched his latest with a victory in Thailand in October 2019. There were still four races to go in the season! He ended up with 12 wins on the year.

Eli Tomac

The Bruins led the way when the NHL called time-out on the season.

NHL 2019–20

Like all other team sports, the NHL had to shut down early. The last game was played on March 11. The regular season had been scheduled to end on April 4. In late summer, the NHL hoped to hold a Stanley Cup tournament that ended after we printed this book. Before the shutdown, though, fans had enjoyed some great games.

In the Eastern Conference, the Boston Bruins skated ahead of the pack. They were led by high-scoring right wing **David Pastrnak**. After a slow start, the Tampa Bay Lightning started to show the form that has made them a powerhouse. Close behind were the Washington Capitals and surprising Philadelphia Flyers. When the season stopped on March 12, only three points separated teams for second place.

In the West, the St. Louis Blues, the 2019 Stanley Cup champs, were atop the standings. They led the young Colorado Avalanche by just two points. Colorado fans were watching breakout seasons center **Nathan MacKinnon** and rookie defenseman **Cale Makar**.

HOCKEY NOTES

Young Stars:
Jack Hughes from Florida and **Kaapo Kakko** from Finland were the top draft picks before the 2019–20 season. Hughes ended up with the New Jersey Devils. Kakko was picked by the Devils' rival, the New York Rangers.

Lots of Tkachuks:
The stands were full of **Tkachuks** (say, "kah-CHUK") on January 18, 2020, in Ottawa when the Senators played the Calgary Flames. Tkachuk brothers **Matthew** (Calgary) and **Brady** (Ottawa) faced off. Their famous dad is **Keith Tkachuk**, who played 18 years in NHL and retired in 2010. Referee **Wes McCauley** had a little surprise for the big family at the start of the game. He asked the Tkachuk brothers to do the opening face-off.

Goal-Scoring Machine:
Washington Capitals captain **Alexander Ovechkin** scored his 700th regular-season NHL goal on February 22, 2020, against the New Jersey Devils. He was the quickest to go from 600 goals to 700. "Ovi" took just 154 games. He was also the second quickest to get to 700. He did it in his 1,144th game—only **Wayne Gretzky** needed fewer (886 games).

2020 NHL Champ
Did you watch the NHL playoffs? They were awesome (we assume!). Write the name of the Stanley Cup champion here.

_____

Zamboni Driver + Goalie!

Though the Hurricanes led 3–1, things were not looking good against the Maple Leafs in a game in Toronto. Goalie **James Reimer** was injured and left the game in the first period. Backup goalie **Petr Mrazek** was hurt in the second period. Most teams travel with only two goalies. What now?

Bring in the Zamboni driver! Each NHL home team has an emergency goalie at each game. In Toronto, the lucky guy was **David Ayres**, an arena employee who drove the ice-cleaning Zamboni machine. Ayres was 42 and had only played amateur and college hockey. But he was ready when called and suited up, entering the game to the cheers of the crowd.

Ayres allowed goals on the first two shots he faced. But then be stopped a shot, and blocked seven more. He was the oldest goalie to win his NHL debut game when the 'Canes won 6–3. His unlikely success story made world headlines.

2020 Winter X Games

The Winter X Games were held in Aspen, Colorado, in January 2020. That's old news: It was the nineteenth year in a row that Aspen hosted the X Games. Still, the people who run the Games always have something new to keep the action moving. The 2020 X Games slate included new jam sessions in the SuperPipe and Slope Rail, plus the debut of the Ski Knuckle Huck.

A great last run gave Castellet the gold.

¡Viva España!

With Americans **Kelly Clark** (retired) and **Chloe Kim** (studying at Princeton) not on the scene in Aspen, it was time for someone else to step up in Women's Snowboard SuperPipe. Spain's **Queralt Castellet** won the battle for the top spot. She rallied to win on the last run! At 30, the oldest snowboarder in the field, Castellet won her first X Games gold medal.

With the Greatest of Ease

Scotty James flew through the air in the Snowboard SuperPipe! He soared 15 feet, nine inches above the rim on his gold medal–winning final run. That gave him 10 victories in a row in halfpipe events around the world. It also was his second straight gold medal in the X Games. James's clinching run included a switch backside double 1260.

18

That's the record-tying number of Winter X Games medals for **Mark McMorris** after he took home silver in the men's Snowboard Big Air competition in Aspen. McMorris, who equaled legendary **Shaun White's** career total in Aspen, then broke the mark in the same event at the X Games in Norway later in 2020.

TEEN SENSATION

Estonia native **Kelly Sildaru** had a busy January in 2020. Fresh off a gold medal–winning performance at the Winter Youth Olympics in Switzerland, she added gold medals at the X Games in the Ski Slopestyle and Ski SuperPipe. Her winning run in the Slopestyle was awesome, with three different 900s—that's 2.5 spins in the air. In Aspen, the 17-year-old tied **Shaun White** and **Nyjah Houston** for the most career X Games medals (nine, including five golds) by a teenager.

Sildaru soared to gold!

BEST IN SNOW

Another new wrinkle for 2020 was the Best in Snow award. It was given to the most memorable performer at the Games. **Colby Stevenson** won when he became the first X Games rookie to win gold in the Ski Slopestyle. He was also the first rookie to win two golds in his X Games debut (number two was in Ski Knuckle Huck).

Winter Sports

World Cup Skiing

Mikaela Shiffrin is fast becoming a skiing legend. She's a three-time World Cup champion! In 2019–20, she won six World Cup races to bring her career total to 66. Though only 25, she ranks fourth on the all-time list. Sadly, her season ended in February 2020 when she had to rush home to see her dad, who had been injured. He later died of his injuries.

With Shiffrin out, **Federica Brignone** became the first female Italian skier to win the overall World Cup title. The season ended two weeks early, in March. Brignone also was the individual champ in the Giant Slalom and Alpine Combined. On the men's side, **Aleksander Aamodt Kilde** of Norway won his first overall championship, even though he didn't win any individual titles.

Viva Italia! Brignone was No. 1.

Cool As Ice

Alysa Liu took the ice for her final routine at the 2020 US Figure Skating Championships. She had to wait a moment, because the crowd was still on its feet. They were cheering **Mariah Bell**, Liu's closest rival. But Liu didn't get rattled. "Okay," she thought, "she did well and now I have to do well." That's a pretty calm reaction for anyone in the heat of a fierce competition. Now consider that Liu was only fourteen years old! The 2019 US champ made it back-to-back crowns. Liu, Bell, and third-place finisher **Bradie Tennell** earned Olympic spots for 2022.

Nathan Chen won the men's national title. The 2018 Olympic bronze medalist was the first man in more than three decades to win four US championships in a row.

In the pairs figure skating event, the husband-and-wife team of **Chris Knierim** and **Alexa Scimeca Knierim** took home the gold and qualified for the next Olympics, too.

Alysa Liu

Rugby World Cup

Every four years, the best national rugby teams compete for the Webb Ellis Cup at the Rugby World Cup. The trophy is named for **William Webb Ellis**, the British student who, according to legend, first picked up a football (a soccer ball to Americans) and ran with it, inventing the sport of rugby in 1823.

Ninety-three countries competed for the 20 spots in the World Cup field in Japan in 2019. The United States qualified when it beat Canada way back in the summer of 2017. But the Americans, who had the thirteenth-ranked team in the world, struggled when they got to Japan. The US lost all four of its games and was eliminated in group play. Japan breezed through pool play with four victories, but the tournament host fell to South Africa in the opening knockout round.

SEMIFINALS
England 19, New Zealand 7

England, the nation that was the birthplace of rugby, earned a spot in its first World Cup final since 2003 by beating a team that had not lost a World Cup match in 12 years! England beat the famous All Blacks from New Zealand 19–7. **George Ford** made four penalty kicks, while England's defense shut down the speedy and powerful Kiwis.

South Africa 19, Wales 16

A hard-fought game turned on a late penalty awarded to South Africa. A backup kicker, **Leigh Halfpenny**, booted one through with four minutes left. The Springboks played tough defense to the end to keep Wales from tying the game or going ahead.

FINAL
South Africa 32, England 12

For the third time, South Africa took home the Webb Ellis Cup. For the first time, though, the team's captain was a black man. South Africa continues to battle racism and division, and the team's win was seen as a sign of hope and unity. **Siya Kolisi** and his team raced to a 12–0 halftime lead, then never let England get close in the second half. **Handre Pollard** scored 22 points on penalty kicks and conversions.

Kolisi joyously raised a historic Cup.

Golf 2019-20

Like just about everything else on the sports calendar, golf's 2020 season was unlike any other in its history. Nothing was stranger than seeing the Masters, traditionally the highlight of every golf fan's spring, shifted to November! The British Open for 2020 was canceled altogether for the first time since World War II. Before golf was forced into a three-month time-out, the PGA Tour produced some memorable highlights. And in late 2019, before the crisis, the best in the world played in major team competitions.

Tiger's team took home the trophy!

Presidents Cup

With a final-day comeback in Australia, the US team won the 2019 Presidents Cup over a team of all-stars from around the world. (The all-star team doesn't include players from Europe. America plays Europe in the Ryder Cup, which came again in fall 2020—perhaps!) **Tiger Woods**, the captain of the US Presidents Cup team, showed the way with three match victories. The Americans began the final day of competition down 10–8. But Woods began that day with a win over **Abraham Ancer**. That was the first of a record-tying eight wins in the twelve singles matches. **Matt Kuchar's** five-foot birdie putt in a match against **Louis Oosthuizen** clinched the eighth Presidents Cup title in a row for the US.

Solheim Cup

Europe's best female golfers rallied from behind in Scotland to capture the 2019 Solheim Cup against a team of top US players. **Anna Nordqvist** of Sweden, **Bronte Law** from England, and **Suzann Pettersen**, another Swede, won the last three singles matches of the final day. That gave them winning points in a 14.5–13.5 victory. Pettersen sank a six-foot birdie putt to beat **Marina Alex** and start a big celebration. Pettersen (right), a 15-time winner on the LPGA Tour, then announced her retirement from pro golf. "I think this is the perfect end for my career," she said. "It doesn't get any better, and to do it with these girls is amazing." It was the first time Europe had won the event, held every two years, since 2013.

GOLF NOTES

TIGER IS NO. 1!

Well, tied for number one, anyway. With a win in the inaugural Zozo Championship event played in Japan in October 2019, **Tiger Woods** tied Sam Snead's record of eighty-two career PGA Tour victories. How times have changed: Snead won a total of $192,000 for ALL of his victories. Woods earned $1.75 million for this win alone!

MR. FIFTEEN MILLION

When the PGA Tour schedule was halted in 2020, **Rory McIlroy** was the No. 1 ranked men's player in the world. We could give you fifteen million reasons for that—the amount of money he received for winning the FedEx Cup championship for 2019. The FedEx Cup featured a unique format that season. Players entered the final tournament, the Tour Championship, with a starting score in relation based on their place in the season-long standings. McIlroy was fifth in the standings to that point. So before he teed off on the first hole of the Tour Championship, he stood five shots behind the leader, **Justin Thomas**. No problem! Over the next four days, McIlroy was the only player in the 30-man field to shoot each round in the sixties. He won by four shots.

AMERICAN DREAM

Swedish native **Annika Sorenstam** came to the United States as a teenager in 1990 to play golf at the University of Arizona. Three decades later, by then an American citizen and one of the best professional female golfers in history, she was selected

McIlroy drove home with a huge prize!

to receive her adopted country's highest civilian honor: the Presidential Medal of Freedom. She'l get the award at a White House ceremony as soon as such events can be scheduled again. She was the first LPGA player, and the first female athlete who is a naturalized American citizen, to receive the award.

CHIP SHOTS

Longtime rivals **Tiger Woods** and **Phil Mickelson** went head-to-head in May. Woods paired with Pro Football Hall of Fame quarterback **Peyton Manning**, while Mickelson joined future Hall of Famer **Tom Brady**. Woods's team won and the event raised $20 million for COVID-19 relief . . . Tour pro **Joel Dahmen** shot anamazing 58 in a round at his hometown course in Mesa, Arizona . . . European Tour player **Matthias Schwab** hit the ultimate moving target in his native Austria. As Schwab teed off, a drone zipped by overhead to follow his ball flight. But the drive plunked the drone—which kept on all the way to the bottom of a nearby lake!

Tennis 2019-20

Serbia's **Novak Djokovic** and Australia's **Ashleigh Barty** were the top-ranked male and female tennis players in the world when play was halted in the spring of 2020. An American woman, **Sofia Kenin**, made one of the biggest splashes with an upset win at the Australian Open in January.

Andreescu pounded out a US Open win.

Old . . . and New

At the 2019 US Open No. 2 seed **Rafael Nadal** and No. 15 seed **Bianca Andreescu** won the singles titles in that season's final Grand Slam event. It was Nadal's fourth US Open championship and his nineteenth career Grand Slam title, just one behind **Roger Federer's** all-time record.

The nineteen-year-old Andreescu, on the other hand, had never won a Grand Slam title. She shocked American **Serena Williams** in straight sets in the final. Andreescu became the first Canadian to win a Grand Slam singles championship.

NEW GREEK STAR

Spain's Nadal won two Grand Slam titles in 2019 and closed the year ranked No. 1 in the world for the fifth time. However, in a surprise, **Stefanos Tsitsipas** of Greece took the big prize at the season-ending ATP Finals in London. The ATP Finals feature the world's top eight male players. Tsitsipas beat **Dominic Thiem** of Austria in a tiebreaker in the final set of the title match to win his biggest championship yet.

Dream Season

Australia's Barty capped a career year in 2019 by winning the season-ending WTA Finals among the top eight women's players. Barty beat **Elina Svitolina** of Ukraine in the championship match. Barty ended the season ranked No. 1.

Surprise ... and Not

Sofia Kenin entered the Australian Open in January 2020 as the No. 14 seed and with just three career titles. But the 21-year-old American cruised to a surprise title. She lost only two sets the entire tournament. Kenin beat top-seeded **Ashleigh Barty** of Australia in the semifinals, then downed **Garbiñe** Muguruza in the final. She became the youngest American to win a Grand Slam title since 20-year-old **Serena Williams** in 2002.

While Kenin's victory was a surprise to most tennis fans, **Novak Djokovic**'s win on the men's side was not. When the Serbian star beat Austria's **Dominic Thiem** in the final, he won the Australian Open for the eighth time.

ATP CUP

Before the Australian Open got underway, men's teams from 24 nations competed at various sites around the country in the inaugural ATP Cup. Serbia edged Spain in Sydney in the final, with **Novak Djokovic** (below) giving his country a key victory in singles over **Rafael Nadal**. The tournament was a big hit Down Under. Nearly a quarter-million fans attended the matches in Sydney, Brisbane, and Perth. ATP Cup innovations included a unique "Team Zone" in the back end of the court. Unlike any other tournament, players and coaches could confer, strategize . . . and celebrate!

Esports

Esports took center stage while most of the rest of the sports calendar was on hold in 2020. Some big live audience events were affected, but the competition went on. The Electronic Sports League held events in different places. They had to prevent people with faster Internet speeds from getting an advantage! Other leagues played to empty arenas but were streamed to record audiences around the world.

LEAGUE OF LEGENDS

In 2019, four million people watched the League of Legends World Championship on ESPN. ESPN then showed all five matches in the 2020 League of Legends Championship Series Spring Split Playoffs in April. Cloud 9 won its third title in that event. It would have represented North America in the 2020 Mid-Season Invitational in the summer, but that competition was canceled due to COVID-19. Even esports could not resist the virus!

Players Gotta Play

Even before the COVID-19 crisis appeared, esports viewership was way up over 2019. When major pro sports stopped, fans and sponsors turned online gaming in a big way. League of Legends matches were shown on ESPN2. Twitch viewers doubled from March to April 2020. Many pro sports leagues and athletes scratched their competitive itch by powering up.

The Show ...and More

Play Ball? Nope. Play video games? Yup!

Devin Booker

✳ **MLB:** Players from all 30 MLB teams squared off in a 29-game MLB The Show league. Rays pitcher **Blake Snell** went a league-best 24–5 during the regular season. He won seven of eight playoff games to take The Show title.

✳ **NBA:** Nets superstar **Kevin Durant** was the biggest name in a 16-team, NBA 2K20 players' tournament. Phoenix guard **Devin Booker** won the event.

✳ **NFL:** In May, gamers and superstars went head-to-head in Call of Duty: Warzone. NFL players past and present, including Hall of Fame receiver **Terrell Owens**, teamed with members of the Florida Mutineers of the Misfits Gaming Group to benefit COVID-19 relief.

iRacing

NASCAR was one of the first pro sports groups to turn to esports in 2020. The stock-car series built a two-month iRacing schedule. The virtual races were modeled after canceled "real life" events. **Denny Hamlin** won the first on an electronic Miami track. Then he won the last, at a North Carolina "oval."

All the races (screen shot shown below) were televised. The drivers loved the action. "It's extremely realistic," NASCAR star **Clint Bowyer** said. "You're using the same mechanics, the same forces, the same movements as you use in real life to make your car go fast."

Formula 1 Racing didn't miss a chance to hit the virtual track, either. F1 launched a Virtual Grand Prix series beginning with an event "in" Bahrain in March.

DECADE IN SPORTS

The 2010s were packed with sports highlights. We met new heroes, saw new champs, and witnessed events that changed sports (and maybe, a little bit, the world). Since 2020 couldn't fill us up with sports, we went into the Sports Time Machine to remember the past ten years. What was your favorite memory of the past ten years in sports? We're sure you'll find it in here, but also help you re-discover why we all love sports so much!

2010

WINTER GOLD!
Evan Lysacek was the first reigning men's world champion to win Olympic gold since 1988. He beat out Russian Evgeni Plushenko's quadruple jump at the Winter Games in Vancouver.

We'll kick off our look back at the decades with some kickoffs! The Green Bay Packers continued their team's long championship tradition with a win in Super Bowl XLV for the 2010 NFL title. Aaron Rodgers led the way as the Pack won its 13th NFL title and fourth Super Bowl, 31–25 over the Pittsburgh Steelers. And speaking of kicks, college football's championship game ended with one. Auburn's Wes Byrum nailed a 19-yard field goal on the final play to give the Tigers a 22–19 win over Oregon. Heisman Trophy winner Cam Newton capped off his super season by hoisting the title trophy.

Super Aaron!

Sticking with college, the men's and women's NCAA hoops tournaments ended with familiar teams on top. Duke won its fourth national title for the men. The Blue Devils had to overcome super-Cinderella Butler. Butler's Gordon Hayward missed a half-court shot by inches as the buzzer sounded. On the women's side, Connecticut not only won it all—they won them ALL. The Huskies went 39–0, capping their season with a win over Stanford.

Spain's Rafael Nadal dominated tennis, winning three Grand Slams. Serena Williams also won a pair of majors. In golf, Phil Mickelson won his third Masters tournament. Plus, we had the 2010 Winter Olympics! Read more on page 130.

BIG MOMENTS

In baseball, a perfect game happens when a pitcher does not allow a single baserunner and wins the game. It's very rare; through 2019, only 23 have ever been thrown. In 2010, baseball saw two perfect games for the first time since 1880! **Dallas Braden** of Oakland and **Roy Halladay** of Philadelphia pitched their gems in May.

World Sports Highlight

The biggest event in 2010 was the FIFA World Cup, which was held in South Africa. Spain won its first-ever title in this quadrennial (that means every four years) soccer superfest, beating the Netherlands in a tense final. A highlight for US fans came when star midfielder **Landon Donovan** scored very late to beat Algeria 1–0 and send the United States into the Round of 16.

More 2010 Heroes

→ **Jonathan Toews** led the Chicago Blackhawks to the team's first Stanley Cup title since 1961.

→ Skier **Lindsey Vonn** won her third straight World Cup overall championship and was named the Associated Press Female Athlete of the Year.

→ The Iditarod is the world's longest and toughest sled-dog race. On the course up in Alaska, **Lance Mackey** steered his team to its fourth straight win.

→ The marvelous American surfer **Kelly Slater** won his tenth ASP world title.

→ **Cristie Kerr** moved to the No. 1 ranking in women's golf. She became the first American on top since 2004. Her season included a win at the LPGA Championship.

Vonn retired in 2019 with an incredible 82 World Cup event wins, by far the most for a woman.

NBA

Lakers vs Celtics in the NBA Finals. Game 7. Who could ask for more? The two ancient rivals met for the 12th time to determine the NBA champ. Led by Finals MVP **Kobe Bryant** (left), the Lakers won their 16th title with an 83–79 win. It was Bryant's fifth NBA title. His coach, **Phil Jackson** made it an all-time record No. 11; he previously won six with the Chicago Bulls.

WNBA

The Seattle Storm lived up to its name. They "stormed" through the season AND the playoffs! After posting the league's best record, they kept rolling in the postseason. They beat the Los Angeles Sparks and then knocked off the Phoenix Mercury. They swept Atlanta in the Finals. League MVP **Lauren Jackson** also won the Finals MVP trophy.

MLB

The 2010 World Series was going to make history no matter who won. Either the AL's Texas Rangers would win their first, or the Giants would win their first since moving to San Francisco in 1958. In five games, led by pitcher **Tim Lincecum**, the Giants brought home the trophy. SS **Edgar Renteria** had a pair of homers to earn Series MVP honors.

2010 Winter Olympics

One thing you need for sure for a Winter Olympics: snow! Around Vancouver, Canada, that's not usually a problem, but in 2010, the snow was lighter than usual. Thanks to some fast work by snow machines, the Games went on!

❄ Canada won the men's hockey gold medal in front of its home fans. The final win over the United States came in dramatic fashion, as **Sidney Crosby** scored the "golden goal" in overtime.

❄ American **Evan Lysacek** (page 126) won figure-skating gold. **Yuna Wen** of South Korea set a Winter games scoring record in winning the women's gold.

❄ Canada set a record with 14 gold medals, the most by one country at a Games. **Alexandre Bilodeau** won the first of those in moguls.

❄ Shaun White of the US won his second straight half-pipe snowboarding gold. **Kelly Clark** got her first for the women.

❄ Short-track speed skater **Apolo Anton Ohno** skated into the history books with two bronzes and a silver. That gave him a career total of eight Olympic medals, the most by an American in Winter Games history!

Ohno? Oh, yes! The speedskater became an all-time Olympic hero!

2010: THE WINNERS

WORLD SERIES
S.F. Giants

SUPER BOWL
Green Bay Packers

NBA
L.A. Lakers

WNBA
Seattle Storm

NHL
Chicago Blackhawks

MLS
Colorado Rapids

NCAA FOOTBALL
Auburn

NCAA BASKETBALL (M)
Duke

The Blackhawks brought home the Stanley Cup.

NCAA BASKETBALL (W)
Connecticut

NASCAR
Jimmie Johnson

FORMULA 1
Sebastian Vettel

INDYCAR
Dario Franchitti

2011

AGGIES ON TOP!
Texas A&M won the first women's college basketball title in its history. They beat Notre Dame in the final. ND had made its own history earlier in the tournament. They had beaten Connecticut to snap the Huskies' then-record 90-game winning streak!

Denver's Tim Tebow.

Passes and passion marked the championships of the NFL and college football. In the pros, quarterbacks went wild. Three QBs topped 5,000 yards passing—**Drew Brees**, **Matthew Stafford**, and **Tom Brady**. NFL passers had 121 games with 300 passing yards or more. And teams piled up 11,356 points. And Green Bay's **Aaron Rodgers** posted a 122.5 passer rating. All of those were all-time NFL records. So it was not surprising that the Super Bowl turned on a key pass.

Though the New York Giants finished only 9–7, they made it to the big game against the favorite New England Patriots. The Giants hung tough in the game, and trailed by three with three minutes to go. **Eli Manning** led an 88-yard drive toward a go-ahead score. He hit **Mario Manningham** with a 38-yard pass that soon led to the winning TD run by **Ahmad Bradshaw**.

And no memory of 2011 would be complete without a mention of **Tim Tebow**. The former college star came back to lead Denver to the playoffs with a batch of comeback wins, igniting a nationwide frenzy for "Tebow Time."

In college football, Alabama got revenge on LSU for a defeat earlier in the season. In the BCS title game, the Crimson Tide blanked the Tigers 21–0. Kicker **Jeremy Shelley** was perfect on five field goals to lead the way.

BIG MOMENTS

Golfer **Rory McIlroy** was way down . . . and then way up. At the Masters in April, he had a four-shot lead on the last day. Then he shot 80 and lost! Then at the US Open in June, the Northern Ireland star crushed it. He set a record for lowest overall score at 268 and won by eight strokes! What a comeback!

World Sports Highlight

You might not have seen this match, but more than a billion people around the world tuned in for the final of the Cricket World Cup. India defeated Sri Lanka to win its first-ever world title in that nation's favorite sport. The cherry on top? The match was played in India in front of hometown fans!

More 2011 Heroes

→ The Phillies' **Roy Halladay** threw the second no-hitter in MLB postseason history. He blanked the Reds 4–0 in the NL Division Series. (The first such no-no? **Don Larsen's** famous perfect game in the 1956 World Series.)

→ Japan earned a shocking upset of the US women's soccer team in the Women's World Cup. **Homare Sawa** scored with just three minutes left in the game to force a tie. Japan then won in penalty kicks for its first world title.

→ Skateboarder **Nyjah Huston** was just 16 when he swept several big events in 2011. In August, he won a competition that earned him $200,000—the biggest prize yet in action sports!

→ Speaking of action, snowboarder **Kelly Clark** became the first woman to nail a 1080 on the halfpipe during the Winter X Games. Yup, she won the gold!

→ Golfer **Yani Tseng** became the first player from Taiwan to win Golfer of the Year. At 22, she was also the youngest ever to earn five major wins in a career; she got two of them in 2011.

Tseng posed with her LPGA Championship trophy.

Dirk said, "Danke!"

NBA

The Dallas Mavericks won their first NBA title, beating **LeBron James** and the Miami Heat in six games. Dallas was led by **Dirk Nowitzki**, the German-born superstar. Even at 7 feet, Nowitzki had a soft outside shot and great moves. The NBA playoffs included a shocking No. 8 over No. 1 seed, with Memphis surprising San Antonio. One of the NBA's favorite players, **Shaquille O'Neal**, called it a career. He was called "The Big Aristotle," "The Diesel," "Shaq Fu," and a bunch of other cool nicknames.

WNBA

The WNBA turned 15 in 2011 and got a champion for the ages. The Minnesota Lynx won the team's first title—it would be the first of four in the coming decade. They were led by rookie sensation **Maya Moore**, a former University of Connecticut superstar. The Lynx set a team record with 27 wins and swept the Atlanta Dream in the finals to carry home the crown.

NHL

Hockey fans in Boston had waited almost 40 years for their team to bring home the Stanley Cup. In 2011, their wait was over! The Bruins survived a tough playoff road on the way. It took three overtime victories to beat Montreal in an early round. In the Final, Boston needed all seven games to beat the Vancouver Canucks.

No Djok!

Novak Djokovic of Serbia dominated men's tennis in 2011. He got off to a hot start, winning 41 straight matches. And he never cooled off. He captured the season's first Grand Slam in the Australian Open. During Wimbledon in June, he moved to the world No. 1 spot after a semifinal win. In the championship, he knocked off **Rafael Nadal** for his second Grand Slam of the year. He then beat Nadal in the final of the US Open to make it three for four. Only a Nadal win at the French Open prevented Djokovic from achieving the rare Grand Slam of all four titles. Along the way, he also won six events on the ATP Tour. It was an incredible coming-out party for an athlete who has since joined Nadal and **Roger Federer** at the very top of tennis history.

It's not a stretch to call Djokovic a superstar!

2011: THE WINNERS

WORLD SERIES
St. Louis Cardinals

SUPER BOWL
New York Giants

NBA
Dallas Mavericks

WNBA
Minnesota Lynx

NHL
Boston Bruins

MLS
LA Galaxy

NCAA FOOTBALL
Alabama

NCAA BASKETBALL (M)
Connecticut

NCAA BASKETBALL (W)
Texas A&M

NASCAR
Tony Stewart

FORMULA 1
Sebastian Vettel

INDYCAR
Dario Franchitti

Stewart finished out in front in NASCAR.

2012

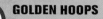

GOLDEN HOOPS
LeBron James led the US men's team to yet another gold medal at the 2012 Summer Olympics in London. The US women won their fifth in a row, too. For more golden highlights, check out page 144.

The biggest championships in American sports saw some similar winners in 2012. In Super Bowl XLVII, the Baltimore Ravens won their second NFL title. They scored first against San Francisco and then held off the Niners every time they tried to catch up. After going up 28–6, Baltimore let San Francisco get close at 31–29, but closed it out to bring home the Lombardi Trophy 34–31. QB **Joe Flacco** had three TD passes to lead the way.

College football football saw another repeat champ. But while Baltimore waited a dozen years to get another trophy, Alabama went back-to-back. The Crimson Tide beat Notre Dame 42–14 in the BCS Championship. They were the first two-in-a-row champs since 2004. RB **Eddie Lacy** was the big star, rumbling for 140 yards and the game's first TD. The title was the 15th for Alabama, by most counts the most in college history.

"Super" Joe Flacco

In baseball, the pattern continued. San Francisco won its second World Series in three seasons. They won in 2010 and then swept the Detroit Tigers in 2012. (San Francisco continued its even-year streak with a win in 2014, too!) The Series was a showcase for **Pablo Sandoval**, nicknamed "Kung Fu Panda." He had three homers in Game 1.

BIG MOMENTS

The Knicks were 8–15 and going nowhere. In February 2011, they brought up **Jeremy Lin**. He was the first player from Harvard in the NBA in 50 years. He also had a huge fan base because he was the first NBA star with roots in Taiwan. Lin electrified the sports world by leading the Knicks on a seven-game winning streak. It was "Linsanity!"

World Sports Highlight

The Tour de France is the world's toughest bicycle race. Cyclists pedal for thousands of miles over more than a month of almost-daily races. The first Tour de France was held in 1903. In all those years, British riders have taken part, but never won. That streak ended in 2012, when **Bradley Wiggins** became the first rider from the United Kingdom to end the race wearing the famous yellow jersey.

More 2012 Heroes

→ NASCAR hero **Jeff Gordon** became only the third driver ever to reach 85 career wins. And **Danica Patrick** became the first woman ever with a full-time NASCAR ride.

→ **Shaun White** won his fifth straight Snowboard SuperPipe at the Winter X Games. It was his 12th X Games gold.

→ Spain won its third European Championship in soccer, beating Italy in the final 4–0.

→ A team from Europe surprised a team of US golfers to win the Solheim Cup, the top international event in women's golf. Spanish golfer **Azahara Muñoz** got the Cup-winning points.

→ **Serena Williams** (left) was on top of women's tennis, capturing Wimbledon and the US Open.

→ Europe's top male golfers stormed back on the final day to win the Ryder Cup over the United States.

You'd jump for joy after winning Wimbledon, too!

NBA

When you put three of the best players on the planet on the same team, you sort of expect to win. Miami combined **LeBron James**, **Dwyane Wade**, and **Chris Bosh** and turned "The Big Three" into the big trophy. It was a big bounce-back from a surprise loss in the 2011 NBA Finals to Dallas. Miami won the Finals in five games, sweeping the final four games. James won the Finals MVP to go along with his NBA MVP.

WNBA

Tamika Catchings was named to the Basketball Hall of Fame in 2020. She took a big step on the way there in 2012 when she led the Indiana Fever to a surprising WNBA title. The Fever knocked off defending champ Minnesota in four games. Catchings scored 28 points in the clinching Game 4 and was named Finals MVP.

NHL

The Los Angeles Kings won the first Stanley Cup in team history! They got the final playoff spot but battled through a tough series of playoff wins. They faced the New Jersey Devils in the final. After an overtime win in Game 1, LA got great goaltending from **Jonathan Quick** to win Game 2. They clinched the Cup in Game 6 by scoring three goals in five minutes late in the game.

Three Perfect Games!

A perfect game is one of baseball's rarest events . . . usually. Heading into the 2012 season, only 19 had been thrown since the first way back in 1880. Amazingly, the second was in 1880, too. Only one other season, 2010, had a pair of perfectos until 2012, when, incredibly, THREE pitchers were perfect.

Philip Humber started out the run of perfection. Perhaps no other perfect-game pitcher was more unlikely. He had started just 29 games. He was on his fourth team in five seasons. And after his perfect-game win, he won only four other games. But on April 21, 2012, he was perfect. He shut down Seattle batter after batter. The only excitement came on out the final out. **Brendan Ryan** checked his swing on a 3–2 pitch and the ump called him out. But the ball skipped past the catcher, who had to throw to first to record the final out of a 4–0 win.

In June, **Matt Cain** of the Giants was staked to an early 7–0 lead. That helped him attack every Houston batter and he polished off the season's second "perfecto." Cain struck out 14. He also got a huge defensive play from right fielder **Gregor Blanco** that saved a sure hit.

"King Felix" finished things off. **Felix Hernandez** went by that nickname. The Seattle righty struck out five of the final six Tampa Bay batters and won 1–0. **Jesus Montero** drove in the game's only run in the third inning. Such a game by a former Cy Young winner was not unexpected. That it was the third in 2012 surely was!

"King" Felix Hernandez celebrates after his perfect game.

2012: THE WINNERS

WORLD SERIES
SF Giants

SUPER BOWL
Baltimore Ravens

NBA
Miami Heat

WNBA
Indiana Fever

NHL
LA Kings

MLS
LA Galaxy

Superstar David Beckham led LA to the top.

NCAA FOOTBALL
Alabama

NCAA BASKETBALL (M)
Kentucky

NCAA BASKETBALL (W)
Baylor

NASCAR
Brad Keselowski

FORMULA 1
Sebastian Vettel

INDYCAR
Ryan Hunter-Reay

2012 Summer Olympics

AMERICAN WOMEN

American women were the biggest story of the 2012 Summer Olympics in London. The US team led the way with 104 total medals. However, nearly 60 percent of them went to female athletes, the highest number ever.

Jumpin' Gymnasts

Gabby Douglas became the first American gymnast ever to win both the all-around gold medal and the team gold medal! Let's hear it for the team that also included **Jordyn Wieber**, **Aly Raisman**, **Kyla Ross**, and **McKayla Maroney**.

Record Run

The women's 4x100-meter relay set a new world record while winning the gold medal. **Tianna Madison**, **Allyson Felix**, **Bianca Knight**, and **Carmelita Jeter** sped around the track in 40.82 seconds. Felix ended with three gold medals in sprints and relays.

Hometown Hero

England's **Jessica Ennis** became the "world's greatest female athlete" with her gold in the heptathlon. She powered across the finish line in the final event to the cheers of the London crowd!

First-Time Gold

Kirani James won the first medal ever for the tiny island nation of Grenada. She won the 400-meter run. The first-ever medals in women's boxing were awarded. **Katie Taylor** earned Ireland's only medal of the Games in the lightweight division.

Gabby Douglas

SUPERSTAR! **Usain Bolt** of Jamaica showed why he was the biggest star and biggest name at the London Games. He became the first runner ever to win back-to-back gold in the 100- and 200-meter races. He capped off his incredible Olympic career by leading Jamaica to the gold in the 4x100-meter relay.

22

With four golds and two silvers in swimming, America's **Michael Phelps** extended his Olympic medals record. Seventeen of his 22 medals were gold. (And he added six more medals in 2016!)

Soccer Stars

The US women's soccer team had been disappointed at the 2011 World Cup. They made up for it with a strong performance in London. They won what might have been the match of the tournament in overtime over Canada. **Alex Morgan** (13, right) scored to send the US to the final. There they beat Japan, 2-1, avenging their loss in the World Cup final.

2013

CHAMPS!
Florida State's Kelvin Benjamin caught this TD pass for the winning points with just 13 seconds left in an awesome college football title game. FSU beat Alabama 34–31. It was the school's third national championship.

ometimes sports can be a source of healing. On April 15, 2013, a bomb exploded near the end of the Boston Marathon. Many people were killed or injured. But the deadly day became an inspiration. The Boston Red Sox were among many sports teams that led the "Boston Strong" movement to help the city recover. Beloved Sox star **David "Big Papi" Ortiz** famously told fans, "This is our . . . city!" The Red Sox and their fans rode a wave of courage and strength all the way to the World Series. Boston won its third MLB title since 2004, beating the St. Louis Cardinals.

Big Papi rallied Boston.

College football fans will talk about the 2013 Auburn-Alabama game for years. First, the "Iron Bowl," as it's known, is one of the sport's fiercest rivalries. It has seen tons of great plays and champions, but nothing like this game. With just a few seconds left, the game was tied 28–28. Alabama tried a 57-yard field goal to win it. The kick was short and **Chris Davis** decided to return it. Yes, you can do that! Incredibly, he scored on a 109-yard return to win the game in incredible fashion!

After all that excitement, the Super Bowl was much quieter—except in Seattle, where fans went wild over their Seahawks' first NFL championship. QB **Russell Wilson** led the way as Seattle crushed Denver 43–8.

BIG MOMENTS

The America's Cup sailing races have been held since 1851. The event had never seen anything like the 2013 competition. America's Team Oracle trailed New Zealand by an incredible 8–1 score in race wins. The first team to win nine took home the Cup. In one of the most incredible comebacks ever, Oracle swept to eight wins in a row for the amazing victory.

World Sports Highlight

This should probably be called a "lowlight." American cyclist **Lance Armstrong** had won a record seven Tour de France races. The month-long race is one of sports' greatest tests. However, in 2012, he had his titles taken away. After many years of denial, early in 2013, Armstrong confessed that he had used performance-enchancing drugs many times during his career.

More 2013 Heroes

→ The Chicago Blackhawks won the NHL season that almost wasn't. The players and owners argued about contracts. No games were played in October, November, or December. The season finally started in January and only lasted 48 games. But Chicago earned its Stanley Cup fair and square, beating the Boston Bruins in the six-game final.

→ Double backside alley-oop rodeo. If you know what this is, congrats! For the rest of us, it's the incredible snowboard trick that **Elena Hight** landed. She was the first ever, man or woman, to nail it!

→ **Andy Murray** won the men's Wimbledon singles. Why the big deal? He was the first person from Great Britain to win England's top event since 1936!

→ **Jack Taylor** from tiny Grinnell College put up a pretty huge number. He set an all-time college record by pouring in 138 points in a game. (Yes, Grinnell won.)

→ **Breanna Stewart** led the Connecticut women to their eighth NCAA basketball title. UConn beat Louisville 93–60 in the final.

Huskies again: Stewart was a star for UConn.

NBA

The Miami Heat continued their dominance, thanks to the Big Three of **LeBron James**, **Dwyane Wade**, and **Chris Bosh**. They beat San Antonio in the NBA Finals, but the Spurs made the Heat work. Miami needed a last-second shot by **Ray Allen** to win Game 6. In Game 7, James poured in 37 to seal the title.

WNBA

Swish... and sweep! The Minnesota Lynx made it two titles in three years. They were led once again by **Maya Moore**, who scored 23 points in the final win. Moore was named Finals MVP. Minnesota went on to win two more titles in the decade.

MLS

Ties in championship soccer are not allowed. The game has to end. The solution, which few people really like, is a penalty-kick shootout. The 2013 MLS Cup ended with an epic shootout, though. Sporting Kansas City and Real Salt Lake tied 1–1 before penalties. Then both teams battled through *nine* rounds of PKs before a miss by Salt Lake gave SKC its first MLS championship.

Park Power

Heading into 2013, the LPGA Tour certainly knew who South Korean star **Inbee Park** was. She had won her first women's Major tournament in 2008 when she was only 19. By 2012, she had added several other regular tournament wins. But 2013 was her breakout year. She won five tournaments in the first half of the year, including three Majors: the Kraft Nabisco Championship, the LPGA Championship, and the US Open. Golf fans had to go way back to 1950 and the great **Babe Didrikson Zaharias** to find another golfer who had won the first three women's Majors. Not surprisingly, Park was the leading money-winner for the year and was named LPGA Golfer of the Year.

Comeback City

Phil Mickelson led the 2013 US Open entering the final day. It was familiar territory. He had done the same six other times only to end up losing. Guess what? He did it again in 2013, falling to **Justin Rose** of England. However, in the British Open (right), Mickelson got some revenge. He posted a personal-Grand Slam best 66 to win. It was his fifth Grand Slam win but his first—and only—British Open title.

2013: THE WINNERS

WORLD SERIES
Boston Red Sox

SUPER BOWL
Seattle Seahawks

NBA
San Antonio Spurs

Seattle won its first Super Bowl.

WNBA
Minnesota Lynx

NHL
Chicago Blackhawks

MLS
Sporting Kansas City

NCAA FOOTBALL
Florida State

NCAA BASKETBALL (M)
Louisville

NCAA BASKETBALL (W)
Connecticut

NASCAR
Jimmie Johnson

FORMULA 1
Sebastian Vettel

INDYCAR
Scott Dixon

2014

Eighteen-year-old US slalom skier Mikaela Shiffrin became the youngest Olympic Alpine skiing gold medalist ever. She was a bright spot for the US ski team, which had several of its stars fall to injury or slow times.

The snow turned gold for the Winter Olympics, which were held in Sochi, Russia. American athletes dominated the "action" sports such as snowboarding and the new slopestyle skiing. **Sage Kotsenburg** won snowboard slopestyle. He did it with a trick he had never even tried before! **Jamie Anderson** won the women's gold in the same event. In halfpipe, **Kaitlyn Farrington** kept the US gold run going. Slopestyle skiing combined the aerial action of ramps with skiing. In the sport's first Olympic appearance, Americans swept the medals, thanks to **Joss Christensen**, **Gus Kenworthy**, and **Nick Goepper**.

Dancing to gold!

After **Mikaela Shiffrin** saved the Alpine team's reputation, **Charlie White** and **Meryl Davis** (above) came through in ice dancing. With a beautiful final routine, they captured their first gold. The US also earned a gold in the new team skating event, thanks in part to **Gracie Gold**. The US had not won a bobsled medal of any color for 62 years. That changed when **Steven Holcomb** piloted the two-man sled to a bronze finish. And Canadians celebrated when their ice hockey teams won both the men's and women's gold medals. Finally, here's a tip of the Olympic rings to **Ole Einar Bjoerndalen** of Norway. He won two golds in biathlon. That pushed his career medal total to 13, the most ever by an individual athlete in Winter Games history.

BIG MOMENTS

A great year for Connecticut basketball! In the men's final, UConn faced Kentucky. It was the first title game that matched a No. 7 and a No. 8 seed. Connecticut won 60–54. The women's team had an easier path, remaining undefeated all year. In the championship game, UConn beat Notre Dame 79–58 for a Huskies sweep!

World Sports Highlight

It's not a huge sport in the US, but field hockey is a big deal around the world. In 2014, the Netherlands won the Women's World Cup for a record seventh time. (It probably helped that they were playing in front of home fans!) In the men's event, those fans were not as happy. Australia won the World Cup by defeating the Dutch in the finals.

More 2014 Heroes

- **Dale Earnhardt Jr.**, won his second career Daytona 500. He had won in 2004 but then finished second three times. He finally got his second in a rain-delayed race.

- **Chloe Kim** was only 13 when she earned a snowboarding silver at the Winter X Games. It was a sign of things to come for the future Olympic champ.

- Future Dallas Cowboys star **Ezekiel Elliott** scored four touchdowns as Ohio State whomped Oregon 42–20 to win the 2014 college football championship.

- **Mo'ne Davis** became the first girl to be a starting pitcher at the Little League World Series. She won the game and was the talk of baseball!

- **Erica Enders-Stevens** became the first woman to win drag racing's Pro Stock championship. She was the second woman ever to win any drag-racing title; the first was **Shirley Muldowney** in 1977.

Elliott was a bashin' Buckeye in a win over Oregon.

NFL

Super Bowl XLIX ended in shocking fashion. The Seahawks were one yard away from scoring the winning TD to win their second straight NFL title. But New England's **Malcolm Butler** picked off a **Russell Wilson** pass at the goal line. Most fans thought Seattle should have tried to run. Instead, the Patriots won their fourth Super Bowl and **Tom Brady** earned his third Super Bowl MVP trophy.

NBA/WNBA

The "Big Fundamental" overcame the "Big Three" in the NBA Finals. **Tim Duncan** led the San Antonio Spurs over the Miami Heat's deep lineup. It was the Spurs' fifth NBA title. In the WNBA, powerful star **Brittney Griner** captured her first league title. She and future WNBA all-time leading scorer **Diana Taurasi** led the Phoenix Mercury over the Chicago Sky in the Finals.

MLB

Madison Bumgarner starred for the San Francisco Giants. He won Games 1 and 5 and pitched five innings in relief in Game 7. He earned the save when Kansas City stranded a possible tying run on third base in the ninth. It was the Giants second World Series title in three seasons.

The 2014 World Cup

Howard was the hero with amazing saves like this one.

For the first time, soccer's World Cup was won by a team from outside the host continent. The Cup was played in Brazil (in South America) but Germany (from Europe, of course) came home as champs.

The powerful German team embarrassed the host Brazilians. Their 7–1 victory stunned the soccer-crazy South American team and its devoted fans. Germany rode the momentum of that big win into the final. There they faced the amzing **Lionel Messi** and Argentina. But Messi and his mates could not crack the German defense. In fact, no one scored until extra time. In the 113th minute, **Mario Götze** scored the Cup winner. Messi was named the top player in tournament, but he didn't get the trophy he really wanted.

The American team did better than expected. In the group stage, the US beat Ghana and tied Portugal. Though they lost to Germany, they made it to the next round. In the round of 16 game, goalie **Tim Howard** became a legend. He set a World Cup record with 16 saves, including many incredible diving stops. Belgium won in overtime, though, 2–1, to knock out the Americans.

2014: THE WINNERS

WORLD SERIES
SF Giants

SUPER BOWL
NE Patriots

NBA
San Antonio Spurs

WNBA
Phoenix Mercury

Will "Power"-ed to the IndyCar title.

NHL
LA Kings

MLS
LA Galaxy

NCAA FOOTBALL
Ohio State

NCAA BASKETBALL (M)
Connecticut

NCAA BASKETBALL (W)
Connecticut

NASCAR
Kevin Harvick

FORMULA 1
Lewis Hamilton

INDYCAR
Will Power

2015

The eyes of the sports world were on women's soccer when the 2015 Women's World Cup kicked off in Canada. The US was heavily favored, but they had lost to Japan in the 2011 World Cup, so they had revenge on their minds. The US beat Australia 3–1 in the first game. Goalie **Hope Solo** helped preserve a 0–0 tie against powerful Sweden. A 1-0 win over Nigeria wrapped up the first round.

Trophy time for the US women's team.

Captain **Carli Lloyd** scored the only goal in a 1–0 win over China. Lloyd and **Kelley O'Hara** were the goalscorers in a big semifinal win over Germany.

The final game against Japan was over quickly. The US and Japan played the full 90 minutes, but the outcome was all but certain after only 15. That's because it only took that long for Lloyd's hat trick to spark the US to a 4–0 lead. Her third goal was an all-time classic, a 50-yard strike from near midfield that flew over the shocked goalie's head. When the final whistle blew, it was 5–2 USA!

The American team danced amid the confetti as they celebrated their third world championship.

BIG MOMENTS

A new superstar came out of the 2015 World Swimming Championships. American **Katie Ledecky** became the first female swimmer to win gold medals in the 200-, 400-, 800-, and 1,500-meter freestyle races. She set world records in the 800 and 1,500, too! Add in a gold in the 4x200-meter relay as well! Watch for more Ledecky gold in 2016!

World Sports Highlight

When more than a billion people pay attention to something, it's worth checking out. That many people—and probably more—tuned in to parts of the Cricket World Cup, which was played in Australia and New Zealand. Those two teams loved the home cooking, because they met in the final. The Aussies continued a long domination of the sport, winning their fifth World Cup, 186–183.

More 2015 Heroes

→ Golfer **Jordan Spieth** had a year for the ages. He won the Masters and the US Open and came a stroke short of adding the British Open. He also finished second at the PGA Championship!

→ Skateboard legend **Bob Burnquist** added to his incredible medal total at the 2015 X Games. By capturing two golds, he pushed his record total of medals to 29! He won his first back in 1995!

→ **Chloe Kim** won Winter X Games gold in the Superpipe. At 14, she was the youngest X Games winner ever to that point.

→ Goalie **Corey Crawford** and center **Patrick Kane** led the Chicago Blackhawks to their third Stanley Cup in six seasons, beating the Tampa Bay Lightning in the final.

→ Bobsled driver **Elana Meyers Taylor** became the first American woman to win the World Cup in this winter sport. The World Cup is a season-long competition of eight races.

Spieth had the best year of his life in 2015.

NBA/WNBA

Sharpshooting **Stephen Curry** lit up scoreboards around the NBA. His Golden State Warriors set a team record with 67 wins and earned their first NBA title since 1975. They beat **LeBron James** and the Cleveland Cavaliers in six games. The Minnesota Lynx continued their hot play in the WNBA. They won a thrilling five-game WNBA Finals over the Indiana Fever. It was Minnesota's third title in five seasons.

Curry powered the Warriors to the title.

NFL

The NFL celebrated Super Bowl 50. Denver beat Carolina 24–10, thanks largely to bottling up the Panthers' great QB **Cam Newton**. Broncos LB **Von Miller** was named the game's MVP. His biggest play came on a strip-sack in the fourth quarter that forced a turnover and led to the game-clinching points.

MLB

The Kansas City Royals won the first World Series in team history with a five-game triumph over the New York Mets. Game 1 lasted 14 innings, with the Royals winning 5–4. **Alex Gordon** tied that game in the ninth with a homer, and **Eric Hosmer**'s sac fly in the 14th was the game-winner. KC's solid pitching kept the Mets bats quiet for most of the rest of the way.

Serena Slam

The Grand Slam in tennis means winning the four major tournaments in the same year: the Australian Open, French Open, Wimbledon, and the US Open. In 2015, the great **Serena Williams** invented her own kind of tennis "title." When she won Wimbledon in July, she had four straight Grand Slam wins, dating back to the 2014 US Open, thus creating the "Serena Slam." They didn't come in the same year on the calendar, but no one else had ever matched her four-in-a-row feat!

First in 37

Horses have their own kind of Grand Slam. The Triple Crown includes the Kentucky Derby, Preakness Stakes, and Belmont Stakes. Winning all three is very hard. In 2015, though, **American Pharoah** did it, capturing all three races with **Victor Espinoza** (right) as the jockey.

2015: THE WINNERS

WORLD SERIES
KC Royals

SUPER BOWL
Denver Broncos

NBA
Golden State Warriors

WNBA
Minnesota Lynx

NHL
Chicago Blackhawks

MLS
Portland Timbers

NCAA FOOTBALL
Alabama

NCAA BASKETBALL (M)
Duke

The Royals were the kings of baseball.

NCAA BASKETBALL (W)
Connecticut

NASCAR
Kyle Busch

FORMULA 1
Lewis Hamilton

INDYCAR
Scott Dixon

2016

CUBS WIN!
The last time the Cubs won the World Series, there were only 46 United States and no World Wars. Theodore Roosevelt was just about to be elected the 26th president. We're up to number 45 now. In other words, it had been a loooong time! But in 2016, the long wait for Cubs fans was over.

What a year! We don't have enough pages to cover all the incredible sports events in 2016. Not only was it an Olympic year (see page 170), but fans were treated to upsets, new records, comebacks, and much, much more.

For baseball fans, 2016 will always be the year the Chicago Cubs finally won. Before they beat the Cleveland Indians in a thrilling, extra-inning Game 7, the Cubs had not won the World Series since 1908. That's 108 years, sports fans! But the team finally put together the pieces to retire their curse and make Cubbies fans dreams come true.

Watson was a winner!

Speaking of Cinderella stories, Leicester City was a 5,000-to-1 underdog at the start of the 2015–2016 Premier League season. Led by hot-scoring Jamie Vardy, though, the Foxes stunned the soccer world by winning the championship. It was one of the most shocking surprise titles in sports history.

Back in the US, the college football title for 2016 went down to the final play. Clemson's Deshaun Watson, a future NFL star, hit Hunter Renfrow with a 2-yard TD pass on the game's final play to beat Alabama 35–31.

BIG MOMENTS

The 2016 NBA season was the last for one of the game's all-time superstars. Lakers guard **Kobe Bryant** retired after 20 incredible seasons that saw him win five NBA titles and earn 18 All-Star selections. Kobe went out in style, scoring 60 points in front of his hometown fans. Sadly, Bryant would die in a helicopter crash just four years later (see page 91).

World Sports Highlight

During the 2016 European Championship of soccer (played between nations, not pro teams), Iceland made new fans around the world by winning its group with several big upsets. Then it beat England in the quarterfinals. The "Viking Clap" that its fans performed became a huge hit as the country of only 300,000 nearly became a Goliath.

More 2016 Heroes

→ For the first time, a wheelchair singles tournament was held at the famous Wimbledon courts in England. **Gordon Reid** was the men's champ, while **Jiske Griffioen** won the women's event.

→ New Zealand golfer **Lydia Ko** became the youngest woman ever with two major championships after she won the 2016 ANA Inspiration in April. She was only 18!

→ **Kris Jenkins** of Villanova hit a buzzer-beating three-point shot to win the NCAA men's basketball title. It was only the second time ever that such a shot won the big dance. 'Nova beat North Carolina 77–74.

→ **Carissa Moore** clinched her third world surfing title by capturing the Pipeline Masters in Hawaii.

→ Congrats to the West Indies team that won the cricket T20 World Championships. **Carlos Brathwaite** hit four straight sixes (a six is like a home run) to win the final game.

→ Goalie **Sabrina D'Angelo** made three penalty-kick saves to help her Western New York Flash team win the NWSL title.

Surf's up! Moore shot the curl for the win.

Breanna Stewart capped off a great four years.

NCAA

In the women's basketball tournament, history was made when Connecticut won its fourth title in a row. No other women's team had done that and only UCLA had reached that total in men's hoops. It was title No. 11 overall for the Huskies and capped off a 38–0 perfect season.

WNBA

In a Game 5 that experts called an "instant classic," the LA Sparks hung on to beat the Minnesota Lynx 77–76. Nneka Ogwumike hit a jump shot with 3.1 seconds for the winning points and the Sparks' first title since 2002.

NFL

Tom Brady was already a Super Bowl legend. He added another page to his incredible story by leading his Patriots on a 25-point second-half comeback over the Atlanta Falcons. He drove them to a game-tying touchdown and then in overtime, directed a drive that won the game 34–28.

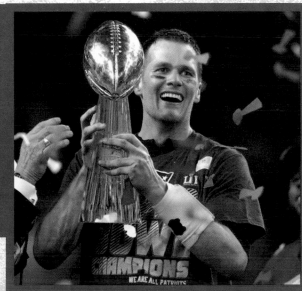

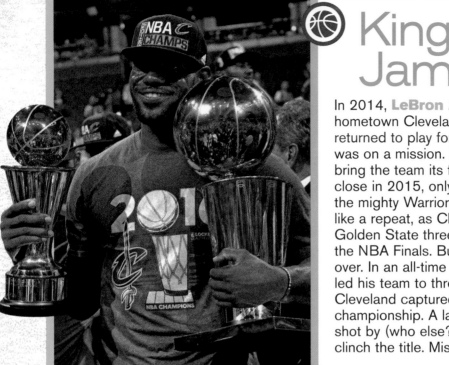

King James

In 2014, **LeBron James** thrilled his hometown Cleveland fans when he returned to play for the Cavaliers. He was on a mission. He badly wanted to bring the team its first title. He came close in 2015, only to be defeated by the mighty Warriors. In 2016, it looked like a repeat, as Cleveland trailed Golden State three games to one in the NBA Finals. But then James took over. In an all-time NBA first, "The King" led his team to three straight wins and Cleveland captured its first-ever NBA championship. A last-minute blocked shot by (who else?) LeBron helped clinch the title. Mission accomplished!

Another King

In NASCAR, **Richard Petty** is "The King." He won seven NASCAR season titles. Later, **Dale Earnhardt Sr.** matched him. In 2016, this exclusive club got a third member. California native **Jimmie Johnson** (right) won the NASCAR title, his seventh since he won his first in 2006.

2016: THE WINNERS

WORLD SERIES
Chicago Cubs

SUPER BOWL
NE Patriots

NBA
Cleveland Cavaliers

WNBA
LA Sparks

NHL
Pittsburgh Penguins

MLS
Seattle Sounders FC

NCAA FOOTBALL
Clemson

NCAA BASKETBALL (M)
Villanova

LA Sparks' Candace Parker and Nneka Ogwumike

NCAA BASKETBALL (W)
Connecticut

NASCAR
Jimmie Johnson

FORMULA 1
Nico Rosberg

INDYCAR
Simon Pagenaud

2016 Summer Olympics

The athletes of the world assembled in Brazil to compete once again for gold, silver, bronze, and history. As always, some of the stories they created became instant legends. Others will be remembered not for gold, but for their pioneering spirit.

GOLDEN MOMENTS

With three all-around world championships, Simone Biles was already considered one of the greatest gymnasts ever. In 2016, she got rid of "one of." She won four gold medals, including the all-around title. She also helped the US team win gold, too.

Speaking of greatest ever, Japan's Kohei Uchimura could be considered tops all-time, too. He won his second straight all-around gold to go with six straight world championships.

In the pool, American swimmers dominated again. Already the greatest Olympian of all-time, Michael Phelps added to his incredible total. He led all swimmers with five gold medals, and added a sixth for good measure. That increased his all-time total to 28 medals and 23 golds, both Olympic records. Meanwhile, Katie Ledecky added to her own growing total. She became the first woman since 1968 to win gold at 200m, 400m, and 800m freestyle at the same Games. She added another gold in a relay.

Katie Ledecky

HOMETOWN HERO

Brazilians are some of the most intense soccer fans in the world. The sport is number one in their country by far. Their national team has won a record five World Cups. Heading into the Games in Rio, Brazil had never won Olympic gold! Thanks to the incredible star **Neymar Jr.**, they changed that in a hurry. Brazil beat Germany in the final in a penalty-kick shootout. Neymar banked in the winning goal.

3

Three is not really a big number. But in this case, it was huge. Jamaica's **Usain Bolt** earned his third gold medal in the 100-meter race. In the 120 years of Olympic competition, no one had ever done that before. Wow!

Groundbreakers

Several athletes celebrated moments that broke new ground in Olympic competition:

▶ **Simone Manuel** won the 100m freestyle swimming event and became the first African American woman with an individual swimming medal.

▶ While helping the US fencing team win a surprise bronze medal, **Ibtihaj Muhammad** (right) became the first US athlete to take part wearing a hijab, the scarf-like head covering worn by devout Muslim women.

▶ Shooting star **Kim Rhode** became the first Olympian to win gold on five different continents! She won at least one gold every year from 1996 to 2016.

2017

GOOOOALLL!

The NWSL's Portland Thorns won their second league championship. Many of the top US women's national team players (like Meghan Klingenberg, pictured) were part of the league. The Thorns were led by American star Tobin Heath as well as top-scoring Canadian star Christine Sinclair.

Sometimes in sports, the best just keep getting better. The Golden State Warriors had been to three straight NBA Finals heading into the 2016–17 season. So what did they do? They added one of the top players in the league to their already-stacked team led by long-distance scoring sensation **Stephen Curry**. **Kevin Durant** signed up with Golden State as a free agent. Durant was a seven-time All-Star at that point but had never won a championship ring. He helped change

Curry and K.D.

that by pouring in points and ripping down rebounds as his new team beat **LeBron James** and the Cleveland Cavaliers in five games.

In chillier news, American skier **Mikaela Shiffrin** won her first overall World Cup title in 2017. She's a slalom expert and was the world leader in that event, and was also second in giant slalom. That gave her enough points to be the first American woman since **Lindsey Vonn** to be No. 1 in the world.

Backup QB **Nick Foles** and the Philadelphia Eagles shocked the NFL when they upset the New England Patriots 41–33 in Super Bowl LII.

BIG MOMENTS

In the NCAA women's basketball semifinal, Mississippi State made history. They beat Connecticut and snapped a 111-game winning streak for the Huskies. **Morgan William** buried a buzzer-beating jumper to seal the win. In the final, South Carolina beat a probably-tired MSU team to win its first national title.

World Sports Highlight

Spanish super-team Real Madrid became the first team since 1995 to win back-to back UEFA Champions League titles. The Spanish team was led by the incredible **Cristiano Ronaldo**, who scored twice in the final game, a 4–1 win over Italy's Juventus. (Future note: In 2018, Ronaldo joined Juventus!)

🏆 More 2017 Heroes

→ Oklahoma City guard **Russell Westbrook** became the second player ever to average a triple-double for a season (double digits in points, scoring, and rebounds). He also set a record for 42 such games.

→ The US women's team won the hockey world championships with a thrilling 3–2 win over archrival Canada.

→ Longtime star golfer **Sergio García** from Spain finally won the Masters in 2017. He beat England's **Justin Rose** in a playoff to earn the famous green jacket.

→ Alabama bounced back from losing in the 2016 final to defeat fellow SEC team Georgia to win the 2017 college football championship, thanks to surprise freshman QB **Tua Tagovailoa**.

→ The Pittsburgh Penguins, led by superstar **Sidney Crosby**, became the first back-to-back Stanley Cup champs since 1998. They beat the Nashville Predators in six games.

Westbrook was Mr. Triple-Double.

⚽ NWSL

Portland Thorns beat the North Carolina Courage to win their second National Women's Soccer League title. Founded in 2013, the NWSL has since become the longest-running women's soccer league in the US.

⚽ MLS

Toronto FC became the first team outside the United States to win the MLS Cup. However, they called on a pair of American stars—**Michael Bradley** and **Jozy Altidore** (in red at left)—to lead them to their 2–0 win over the Seattle Sounders. Altidore scored the game's first goal.

 ## WNBA

Did the Lynx become the first WNBA dynasty? In 2017, they won their fourth WNBA title in eight seasons. The team tied the Houston Comets for most league championships. **Sylvia Fowles** led the way and was named Finals MVP.

SUPER SERENA!

In tennis, the Grand Slam events are the key goal for all the top players each year. Since 1968, when tennis was open to all pro players, the women's career record for Grand Slam titles was 22, by **Steffi Graf**.

Welcome to the new all-time best! **Serena Williams** won the 2017 Australian Open for her 23rd Grand Slam singles title. It was just the latest great moment in the greatest career in women's tennis (and some might say in all of women's sports). Williams's powerful game has swept through just about everyone since she debuted at the age of 14 in 1995. She and her sister **Venus**, who has seven Grand Slams of her own, have revolutionized tennis.

The year 2017 was also memorable for Serena off the court. She became a mom for the first time!

SERENA'S GRAND TOTAL*

Australian Open	7
French Open	3
Wimbledon	7
US Open	6

*Through 2017.

2017: THE WINNERS

WORLD SERIES
Houston Astros

SUPER BOWL
Philadelphia Eagles

NBA
Golden St. Warriors

WNBA
Minnesota Lynx

NHL
Pittsburgh Penguins

MLS
Toronto FC

NCAA FOOTBALL
Alabama

NCAA BASKETBALL (M)
North Carolina

Surprise Super Bowl hero Nick Foles

NCAA BASKETBALL (W)
South Carolina

NASCAR
Martin Truex Jr.

FORMULA 1
Lewis Hamilton

INDYCAR
Josef Newgarden

2018

TRIPLE CROWN!

Winning horse racing's Triple Crown used to be a rare thing. The sport had gone 37 years without one until 2016. Then in 2018, Justify became the second in three years! Jockey Mike Smith steered the colt to the three biggest wins in racing.

France was No. 1!

Soccer earned a field full of headlines in 2018. The men's World Cup was played in Russia. The home team thrilled its fans by making it to the quarterfinals, where they lost in penalty kicks. England also made it to the semifinals, its best showing since it won in 1966. They lost there to Croatia, who went on to face France in the final. France won easily, 4–2, for the nation's second World Cup title.

In the US, a two-year-old MLS team, Atlanta United, shocked the sport. Fans poured into Atlanta's stadium all season long, setting a series of attendance records. The team responded by winning a lot. Forward **Josef Martinez** was the star, setting a single-season record with 31 goals. Atlanta made the MLS Cup, which was played in its home stadium. Local fans set their own record, packing in 73,019 people. They watched their heroes defeat the Portland Timbers 2–0, with Martinez scoring the first goal.

In other pro soccer news, the great Spanish team Real Madrid won the Champions League for the third time in a row. **Cristiano Ronaldo** was the team's big-name star, but another forward, **Gareth Bale**, scored two huge goals in the second half. Ronaldo made news of his own by announcing later in the summer that he was leaving to play for Juventus in Italy.

BIG MOMENTS

Football fans love to see points on the board. So they really loved the Rams-Chiefs Monday Night Football game in November! The final score was an incredible 54–51 in favor of the Rams! It was the first time that two teams had each topped 50 points in the same game. The 105 total points in the game was the third-highest total ever as well.

World Sports Highlight

The high-speed sport of Formula 1 racing is not a huge deal in the US, but it's enormous around the world. In 2018, British driver **Lewis Hamilton** wrote a new page in the sport's long history. He won his fifth drivers' championship in a row. That tied him with Argentine legend **Juan Manuel Fangio** for second-most all time, behind only the great German driver **Michael Schumacher**.

More 2018 Heroes

→ Tiny University of Maryland, Baltimore County (UMBC) became the first No. 16 seed to beat a No. 1 seed in the men's NCAA tournament. They shocked Virginia and won by 20 points, 74–54. Villanova ended up as the tournament champs.

→ In the women's tournament, Notre Dame needed overtime to beat the mighty Huskies from Connecticut. Then they shocked Mississippi State by rallying from 13 down before **Arike Ogunbowale** hit a buzzer beater to seal the championship.

→ **Shohei Ohtani** made history for the LA Angels. Not since **Babe Ruth** had a player hit a homer and won a game as a starting pitcher in the same week.

→ American superstar **Simone Biles** became the first woman to win four straight world gymnastics championships.

→ At Wimbledon, **Kevin Anderson** beat **John Isner** in a match that took more than six and a half hours! **Novak Djokovic** won the tournament.

Ogunbowale hit this championship-winning shot.

NHL

The Stanley Cup was definitely going to a new team. Neither the Washington Capitals nor the Vegas Golden Knights had ever won. The Knights were an amazing Cinderella story. They were the first new North American sports team ever to make it to a final in its first season. The Cinderella run fell short, though, as the Capitals won in five games to bring home the Cup.

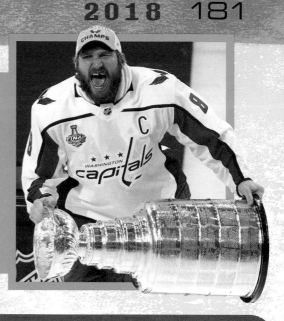

WNBA/NBA

For the first time in NBA history, the same two teams met in the NBA Finals four years in a row. Golden State had beaten Cleveland twice already. In 2018, they made it three titles in four years with a sweep. (Special props to **James Harden** of the Houston Rockets. He scored at least 30 points in 32 straight games, the second-longest streak ever.) In the WNBA, the Seattle Storm did their own sweep over the Washington Mystics.

MLB

The Boston Red Sox became the top World Series team of the 2000s, winning their fourth title since 2004. The Bosox were led by **Mookie Betts**, who became the first player to win a league batting title while also hitting at least 30 homers and stealing at least 30 bases. Boston beat the LA Dodgers in five games.

🥇 2018 Winter Olympics

It's nice when sports can bring people together. The 2018 Winter Olympics were held in PyeongChang, South Korea. Athletes from around the world gathered to compete. Perhaps the biggest news came from North Korea, right next door. For the first time, the North Korean government let athletes walk together with those from South Korea. The two nations have been enemies since 1950! It was a great Olympic moment. Here are some golden moments!

❄️ The Netherlands won an amazing eight gold medals in speedskating, one of their national sports.

❄️ Curling is Canada's national sport, but the US team shocked everyone when it won gold in the icy version of shuffleboard.

❄️ America's **Jessie Diggins** helped the US win its first-ever cross-country gold when she brought home the relay team in first place.

❄️ **Ester Ledecká** of the Czech Republic achieved a "double" first. She was the first athlete ever to win a gold in both skiing (Super-G) and snowboarding (parallel giant slalom) at the same Games.

❄️ Japan's **Yuzuru Hanyu** was the first man to repeat as Olympic figure skating champ since 1952.

❄️ The Games ended on a happy note for the US when the women's ice hockey team won gold. They beat Canada in a shootout after losing the previous three gold-medal games to Canada.

US hockey gold-medal winner Jocelyne Lamoureux

🏆 2018: THE WINNERS

WORLD SERIES
Boston Red Sox

SUPER BOWL
NE Patriots

NBA
GS Warriors

WNBA
Seattle Storm

NHL
Washington Capitals

MLS
Atlanta United FC

NCAA FOOTBALL
Clemson

NCAA BASKETBALL (M)
Villanova

Hamilton won title No. 5.

NCAA BASKETBALL (W)
Notre Dame

NASCAR
Joey Logano

FORMULA 1
Lewis Hamilton

INDYCAR
Scott Dixon

2019

TIGER BURNING BRIGHT
Wearing his traditional final-day red shirt, Tiger Woods celebrated an incredible comeback from injury when he won the 2019 Masters in Augusta, Georgia. It was his fifteenth Grand Slam win, but his first since way back in 2008.

Super Bowl . . . Super Chiefs! QB **Patrick Mahomes** led his Kansas City team to its first Super Bowl since they won Super Bowl IV 50 years ago! Mahomes was the easy choice for 2018 NFL MVP after he threw 50 TD passes in his first season as a starter. But that season ended in playoff disappointment. Mahomes came back with a bang in 2019. His stats were down, but the team's wins were up. Kansas City sent out a great defensive team, while Mahomes kept opponents off-balance with great running and passing. In Super Bowl LIV, Mahomes ran for one TD and threw two TD passes as the Chiefs beat the 49ers 31–20.

Super Patrick!

In the NBA, the Toronto Raptors became the first team outside the United States to win the title. Led by **Kawhi Leonard**, they stormed to victory over the Golden State Warriors in six games to bring the trophy back to Canada. Leonard became the third player to earn NBA Finals MVPs with two teams; he also won that award in 2014 with San Antonio.

BIG MOMENTS

Since he burst onto the scene in the late 1990s, **Tiger Woods** has dominated golf. However, in recent years, injuries and off-the-course problems slowed him down. So when he stormed to victory at the 2019 Masters, golf fans everywhere were thrilled. It was Woods's fifth Master title and his 15th Grand Slam win; that's second all-time behind **Jack Nicklaus's** 18.

World Sports Highlight

Never say die! That's what Liverpool fans were shouting—and their players responded. They needed a probably-impossible four goals against mighty Barcelona to win their Champions League playoff. And that's just what they scored! In the other semi, **Tottenham Hotspur** (in green, below) rallied from three goals down, too, but their rally to beat Ajax was all in the second half!

More 2019 Heroes

- → The Oklahoma women's softball team set an NCAA record by winning 41 games in a row.

- → **Cristiano Ronaldo** led his Portugal team to victory in the first Nations League tournament, held among the top national teams in Europe.

- → **Sabrina Ionescu** became college basketball's all-time triple-double leader. No other male or female player has topped her 13 such games. (She ended her career in 2020 with 24!)

- → **Simon Pagenaud** won the Indy 500 over Alexander Rossi by only two-tenths of a second!

- → **Chloe Kim** won her seventh Winter X Games medal when she captured her fourth Snowboad SuperPipe championship in Aspen.

- → Congrats to England for winning the Cricket World Cup in overtime over New Zealand.

Another trophy for Ronaldo's crowded case!

NHL In late January 2019, the St. Louis Blues were in last place in the NHL. Then they started to turn things around. The Blues earned a playoff spot and stormed through the postseason. In a thrilling Stanley Cup Final, the Blues stopped the Boston Bruins in Game 7 to win the team's first NHL championship.

WNBA MVP **Elena Delle Donne** led her Washington Mystics team to the first championship in team history. In the WNBA Finals, though, Delle Donne was injured. Her teammate **Emma Meesseman** (left) came through, scoring at least 20 points three times as the Mystics beat the Connecticut Sun.

MLB Congrats to the Washington Nationals, who won the first World Series in team history. Though they had the oldest lineup in baseball, the vets came through and beat the Houston Astros in seven exciting games.

⚽ Women's World Cup

The US swamped Thailand 13–0 in the first game. **Alex Morgan** had five goals by herself. Some people thought the US should have let up later in the game. However, the players knew that their goal total was important in the group standings.

How deep was the US? They swapped in seven new players and beat Chile 3–0. **Tierna Davidson**, just 19, had two assists and became the youngest US World Cup player since 1995. The US Team won a tough game against Sweden next to win the group.

Spain scored against the US! That was the big news, as it was the first goal the Americans had allowed. However, **Megan Rapinoe** buried two penalty kicks and the US advanced. In front of a loud French crowd, the American team then beat France 2–1, with Rapinoe scoring two goals.

In the semifinal, the US beat a very good team from England, a 2–1 win highlighted by goalie **Alyssa Naeher** stopping a penalty kick!

In the World Cup final against the Netherlands, Rapinoe kept up her scoring touch with another PK goal. Rising star **Rose Lavelle** scored on a long left-footed shot to double the lead. When the whistle blew, the US had won its fourth World Cup title!

2019: THE WINNERS

WORLD SERIES
Washington Nationals

SUPER BOWL
KC Chiefs

NBA
Toronto Raptors

WNBA
Washington Mystics

Joe Burrow led LSU to the title.

NHL
St. Louis Blues

MLS
Seattle Sounders

NCAA FOOTBALL
LSU

NCAA BASKETBALL (M)
Virginia

NCAA BASKETBALL (W)
Baylor

NASCAR
Kyle Busch

FORMULA 1
Lewis Hamilton

INDYCAR
Josef Newgarden

What's Next?: A Look Ahead

Sports will go on. Don't worry! As of late summer 2020, here's what we hope we can all enjoy in 2021 as sports—and the world—does what it can to get back to normal. Keep an eye on all the league websites and sports media for the latest information.

The Big Asterisk! *All of these dates are subject to change, but we've got our fingers, hockey sticks, baseball bats, and pole vaults crossed!

NFL

▶ Super Bowl LV is planned for Sunday, February 7, 2021 at Raymond James Stadium in Tampa.

NCAA Football

▶ The National Championship Game for the 2020 season is scheduled for January 11, 2021, at Hard Rock Stadium in Miami.

NBA

▶ League hopes to tip off the 2020-21 season in December.

▶ NBA All-Star Game, February 14, 2021, in Indianapolis.

▶ NBA Finals would be in June as usual.

WNBA

▶ The 2021 season should start back on its regular schedule in mid-May.

▶ The 2021 WNBA Finals would be in early October.

MLS

▶ The 2021 season should start in late February.

▶ The 2021 MLS Cup would be held in November in the home stadium of the team with the best record remaining.

NHL

▶ The 2020-21 season hopes to start in late 2020.

▶ The 2021 NHL All-Star Game is scheduled for January 30, 2021, on the home ice of the Florida Panthers near Miami.

▶ The Stanley Cup Final would be in June as usual.

NCAA Basketball

▶ March Madness for 2021 for both the men's and women's tournaments would be in March and April as usual if the seasons start in October 2020.

Summer Olympics

▶ By March 2021, the International Olympic Committee said they would confirm that the postponed Summer Games would take place.

▶ The dates on the table right now are July 23 to August 8 in Japan.

▶ The Paralympics are set to be held August 24 to September 5, also in Japan.

Motor Sports

▶ The 2021 Daytona 500 is scheduled for February 14. The final race for the championship moves to Arizona for the second time. The planned date is November 7.

▶ Formula 1 hopes to drop the flag on a 17-race schedule in late March 2021.

▶ The 2021 Indy 500 is on the calendar for May 30.

Golf

▶ 2021: Masters: April 9-12; PGA Championship May 17–23; US Open: June 14-20; British Open: July 15-18.

▶ 2021: ANA Inspiration: TBA;

Let's hope we can all do this again soon!

US Women's Open: June 3-6; Women's PGA Championship: Date TBA; Evian Championship: July 22-25. Women's British Open: August TBA.

Tennis

▶ Australian Open: Finals, February TBA.

▶ French Open: Finals, June 5 and 6.

▶ Wimbledon: Finals, July 10 and 11.

▶ US Open: Finals, September 11 and 12.

TBA: To be announced

Produced by Shoreline Publishing Group LLC

Santa Barbara, California
www.shorelinepublishing.com
President/Editorial Director: James Buckley, Jr.
Designed by Tom Carling, www.carlingdesign.com

The *Scholastic Year in Sports* text was written by

James Buckley, Jr.

Editorial assistance, including Other Sports and NHL: **Jim Gigliotti**, **Beth Adelman** and **Craig Zeichner**

Fact-checking: **Matt Marini**.

Thanks to team captain Tiffany Colon, the photo squad of Emily Teresa and Marybeth Kavanagh, production pit crew chief Jael Fogle, and the superstars at Scholastic for all their championship work! Photo research was done by the author. This edition was trickier than usual, so the producers really appreciate everyone's extra efforts.

● ●

Photography Credits